May you ex[perience]
the joy
of knowing who He is!
Carolyn Priester Jones
October, 2015

If You Only Knew ...

Who I AM!

by

CAROLYN PRIESTER JONES

Xulon
ELITE

Table of Contents

SECTION ONE: THE POWER OF CHOICE!

SECTION TWO: WHO IS GOD?

SECTION THREE: LIFE IN THE WOMB!

SECTION FOUR: JESUS — GOD WITH US!

SECTION FIVE: THE WAY OF THE CROSS LEADS HOME!

THE ONE

Introduction

*G*od, Jesus and The Holy Spirit are One, together from the beginning of time, together now and together forever.

The Bible is One, from beginning to end. From Genesis through Revelation, God, Jesus and The Holy Spirit speak as One. Verses from different parts of the Bible verify other parts, until it becomes obvious there is One Message. They are not parts, but a Glorious Whole.

The Words of God, Jesus and The Holy Spirit are timeless. Jesus spoke exactly what His Father God said. The Holy Spirit brings to mind what God and Jesus said. What was said in one time in Bible history is verified and repeated in other times. The Word of The Lord said to others in the past is also for us in this time and will be true in time to come.

"I, the LORD, never change. ..."
Malachi 3:6 (GW)

Jesus Christ is the same yesterday, today, and forever.
Hebrews 13:8 (GW)

(Jesus speaking)
"However, the helper, the Holy Spirit,
whom the Father will send in my name, will teach you everything.
He will remind you of everything that I have ever told you."
John 14:26 (GW)

"…but the word of our God will last forever."
Isaiah 40:8 (GW)

(Jesus speaking)
"The earth and the heavens will disappear,
but my words will never disappear."
Mark 13:31 (GW)

As the rain and the snow
come down from heaven,
and do not return to it
without watering the earth
and making it bud and flourish,
so that it yields seed for the sower and bread for the eater,
so is my word that goes out from my mouth:
It will not return to me empty,
but will accomplish what I desire
and achieve the purpose for which I sent it.
Isaiah 55:10-11 (NIV2011)

You are not holding this book by chance. God, Jesus and The Holy Spirit—The Holy One—has sent His Word specifically to you. I believe what He said through the prophet Isaiah—His Word will accomplish what He desires and achieve The Purpose for which He sent it. It has been my privilege to hold the pen and listen to Him. It is my joy to deliver His Word to you.

You are part of the Holy One. God revealed this in His Word, spoken through Jesus. And soon you will know the rest of the story!

"On that day you will realize that,
I am in my Father,
and you are in me,
and I am in you."
John 14:20 (NIV2011)

That day is this day! May you discover with Joy
The One Who lives inside you!

Dedication

I dedicate my life to The One—

My Father God, Creator of the Universe and all that is in it,

Jesus, my Savior, Who brought The Words of Life to me
and ushered me into a LIFE far more wonderful
than I could have ever imagined.

The Holy Spirit, My Advocate and Constant Companion
Who comes in such Power
that I am constantly awed by His Presence.

I praise Them and thank Them for The Life we all live together now
and forever!

Carolyn Priester Jones
June, 2015

Acknowledgments

J thank God for putting me in a family who made it easy to understand God's Love and Grace. I thank God for His Pure Love revealed in all the seasons of the life He gave my parents, Horace and Pearl Priester.

I thank God for giving me a true soul mate in Jay Jones, my husband of 37 years. Using his gift of "added dimension," Jay constantly shows me the Wonders of God's World. His creativity and ingenuity continue to amaze me.

This book was made possible, in large measure, because Jay was willing to use his many, God given talents. Besides sharing his expertise with multi-platform desktop publishing, Jay worked through the many fine details of proof reading, editing and researching.

Jay joined me in prayer for direction and clarity about what to write. He encouraged and challenged me. He asked me questions that sent me searching God's Word for the Answers only He could give.

Most valuable of all was Jay's advice from the first day of writing. "Quote The Word! Don't depend upon any literary skill. The Word speaks for Himself! God will accomplish the Purpose for which He sends His Word."

I thank God for the beautiful life He created in our daughter, Jennifer. Her questions and observations lead me to look deeper. Her persistence and passion for Truth inspire and motivate me.

How to Use This Book

*P*lease pray that The Holy Spirit will reveal to you how He wants you to use this book. God sends His Word to all, but He also sends His Messages in a very personal way to individual people. And He sends His Word at the precise moment He wants to connect.

Therefore, there is no formula for reading this book. The Holy Spirit may guide you to read from the beginning to the end or He may have in mind that you read specific chapters at certain times.

You will find God's Word in every chapter. You will find different verses from different places in the Bible, linked together to illustrate the Consistency of God's Message. You will find some verses, repeated over and over again, but relating to different topics. You will find God's Words, recorded by a variety of authors, but all speaking the same Message God directed them to share.

You will find Biblical Truths proclaimed in ways you may not have considered before now. The Words of this book are intended to help expand your view to see even more of our Awesome God.

You will be encouraged to explore the deeper meanings of common phrases used by Christians, such as "born again," "saved," "sin," and "eternal life."

You will find variety in how the message is presented in this book. You will find the pure Word of God. You will find ideas explored through story format. You will find material suitable for Bible Study. You may find sermon topics. No matter what form the presentation takes, The Message is the same—God knows you and loves you. He wants you to know Him and love Him. He is with you always.

You may find ideas expressed that will affirm what you already believe. There may be information presented that is different from the "Old, Old Story" you grew up with. I challenge you to search God's Word and allow Him to reveal to you His Truth. He will show you exactly what He wants you to know.

> *If any of you needs wisdom to know what you should do,*
> *you should ask God,*
> *and he will give it to you.*
> *God is generous to everyone and doesn't find fault with them.*
> *James 1:5 (GW)*

> *You will seek me and find me when you seek me with all your heart.*
> *Jeremiah 29:13 (NIV2011)*

Many Blessings to you, as you discover Who He is!
Carolyn Priester Jones
June, 2015

The Power of Choice!

…I have set before you life and death,
blessings and curses.
Now choose life,
so that you and your children may live
and that you may love the LORD your God,
listen to his voice, and hold fast to him.
For the LORD is your life …
Deuteronomy 30:19-20 (NIV2011)

Chapter 1

If You Only Knew ...

*T*hroughout time, humans have had a driving desire to know more than what they knew. When we are hungry or thirsty or dissatisfied in any way, we believe it must be because we do not know something. We believe if we knew that "something," we could fix ourselves.

When knowing an abundance of things does not satisfy, we turn to believing if we knew the right person, that gnawing hunger or repeated thirst would go away. That person might be the right boss, the right circle of friends or even the right person to love us. However, even when we have these connections, we sometimes feel empty.

We wonder if our life up to now is all there is. We wonder if it is possible we have missed something. We comfort ourselves with what we believe we know. We are ready to defend to the death the beliefs we have collected over a lifetime. They are our security blanket. We look for things and people to verify what we already believe.

I would like to begin our time together by sharing a story about a woman who believed she understood life. She had had enough hard knocks to make her suspicious of anyone who challenged her. She wasn't prepared for One Who would come to her in humility, simply asking for a drink of water.

She did not know He asked, not to take something from her, but to offer her something far more valuable than what she could give Him. He knew her. He saw beyond what she thought she wanted to what she needed. She did not know Him … yet. But He wanted her to know Him, because He was The Source of a Gift He wanted to give her. That Gift would last her a lifetime.

That day the woman found a Joy she had never known. She found someone who knew her and still loved her. That One knows you and loves you. Maybe you did not know you were searching for Him. But He knew and He is here.

If you knew Who He really is,
You could ask Him any question.
You could ask Him for that which you seek,
and He would willingly give you what you need!

Chapter 2

Will You Give Me A Drink?

*T*he Gospel of John, Chapter 4, Verses 1 through 26 records the story of Jesus' encounter with the woman at the well. This woman had had many experiences with men in her life. No relationship had ever lasted. She had given up on commitment. She was resigned to living in the moment. She knew better than to hope for anything more.

That woman's name is unknown to us. But Jesus, the One Who met her there, knew not only her name, but everything about her. He could have approached her with the Power of His Special Knowledge. He did not. He approached her with respect and in great humility.

> *...Jesus said to her,*
> *"Will you give me a drink?"*
> *John 4:7 (NIV2011)*

Jesus did not demand. She could have said no.

She was a Samaritan. He was a Jew. Jews did not associate with Samaritans. Additionally, He was a stranger. She questioned why He would even talk to her. Jesus answered her.

"If you only knew what God's gift is
and who is asking you for a drink,
you would have asked him for a drink.
He would have given you living water."
John 4:10 (GW)

In that moment, Jesus opened a door that brought her past, present and future into a glorious completion.

The woman believed she knew Who God was. She believed she knew where all the boundaries of His Love were. She believed she understood to what she was entitled and when she might expect to get it. But what little she knew had clouded her view and kept her from receiving the Greatest Love she would ever know.

The woman saw Jesus as only a human with human limitations. If He was proposing to give her something, she was smart enough now to ask questions before going too far into any relationship.

The woman said to him,
"Sir, you don't have anything to use to get water, and the well is deep.
So where are you going to get this living water?
You're not more important than our ancestor Jacob, are you?
He gave us this well.
He and his sons and his animals drank water from it."
John 4:11-12 (GW)

For those of us who grew up in the church, this sounds a bit familiar. When something new is proposed, we often back up and say, "Wait a minute. I know what I was taught all my life. In fact, my parents and grandparents understood the same thing I do. I know the truth already, so don't try to pull anything."

Jesus did not take away her beliefs. He only told her their limits. And He offered to expand her horizons.

24

Jesus answered her,
"Everyone who drinks this water will become thirsty again.
But those who drink the water that I will give them
will never become thirsty again.
In fact, the water I will give them will become in them a spring
that gushes up to eternal life."
John 4:13-14 (GW)

The woman was then willing to receive what she believed Jesus might be able to give her. Not having to come to the well every day and haul water back to the house sounded pretty good to her.

But then Jesus made it personal. Jesus doesn't just run a lemonade stand to cool us off now and then. He wants to give us ongoing food and nourishment.

In order for the woman to know The One, she had to discover she was known by The One, in a way that no mere human could possibly know.

Jesus asked her to bring her husband back to the well with her. She admitted to him the truth. She had no husband. It was at that moment her confession of truth met The Truth standing before her. The One, full of Truth, knew exactly who she was.

…Jesus told her,
"You're right when you say that you don't have a husband.
You've had five husbands,
and the man you have now isn't your husband.
You've told the truth."
John 4:17-18 (GW)

The woman was not ready to address her failings, but she knew she was in the Presence of One Who somehow knew her. She decided He must be a prophet. She acknowledged that. She also acknowledged she knew about worshipping God.

Jesus then told her The Truth about worship.

The Gospel of John, Chapter 4, Verses 23 and 24 records Jesus' Words to her:

"Yet a time is coming and has now come
when the true worshipers will worship
the Father
in the Spirit
and in truth,
for they are the kind of worshipers the Father seeks.
God is spirit,
and his worshipers must worship in
the Spirit
and in truth."
John 4:23-24 (NIV2011)
(Underline added for emphasis)

God, our Father, is ONE, with The Holy Spirit and with Jesus, Who identified Himself as The Way, The Truth and The Life.

Jesus answered him,
"I am the way,
the truth,
and the life. ..."
John 14:6 (GW)

The woman at the well was so close to The Truth and yet, could not grasp the magnitude of the revelation of Truth. She acknowledged to Jesus she knew a Messiah would come one day and explain everything.

Many people today are waiting for Jesus to return one day and explain everything. Jesus then fully revealed Himself to her, as He wants to do for you. We don't have to wait. He is here right now!

Jesus told her,
"I am he,
and I am speaking to you now."
John 4:26 (GW)

Let's go back to the beginning of recorded time when humans first knew God, up close and personal.

Chapter 3

Love Within Boundaries

*G*od, the Creator, loved His First Human Creations, Adam and Eve. He gave them everything they would ever need to enjoy Heaven on earth. God gave them unlimited freedom, except for one important boundary.

> *"But you must never eat*
> *from the tree of the knowledge of good and evil*
> *because when you eat from it, you will certainly die."*
> *Genesis 2:17 (GW)*

Did this mean God would kill them? No. But God knew what would happen if they did eat of the Tree of the Knowledge of Good and Evil. As soon as Adam and Eve stepped out of God's Circle of Protection, they would be subject to the law of sin and death. They would be under the influence of one who hated God, a being now known as satan.

If they remained in obedience to God, they would remain in their heaven on earth, right in the center of God's Love. Obedience and Love are connected intimately. Love has boundaries, not to restrict, but to protect.

Jesus revealed the depths of Love, when He said,

> *"If you love me, you will obey my commandments."*
> *John 14:15 (GW)*

"Whoever knows and obeys my commandments
is the person who loves me.
Those who love me will have my Father's love,
and I, too, will love them and show myself to them."
John 14:21 (GW)

Jesus answered him,
"Those who love me will do what I say.
My Father will love them,
and we will go to them and make our home with them."
John 14:23 (GW)

In one of the most profound secrets revealed to man, Jesus said,

"I can guarantee this truth:
Whoever obeys what I say will never see death."
John 8:51 (GW)

Adam and Eve had the opportunity to avoid ever seeing death. All they had to do was receive God's Boundless Love and live within His One Important Boundary.

But Adam and Eve were about to be tempted to take a peek at death. There was someone else in the garden, who was already anticipating being able to say, "Made you look!"

This creature was created by God to be beautiful and wise. He had been anointed to do God's work. But what he was about to do was not God's Work. It was his own. He had fallen far from what he was created to be. He no longer wanted to serve God. He wanted to be God.

He first needed some human followers. Have a closer look, but be careful. He may look beautiful. He may seem wise. But he bites. And his bite leads to death.

Chapter 4

A Rebellious Cherub

*S*atan, the dungeon master, is called by various names throughout the Bible. Some of those names appear to be names of actual evil kings, through whom satan may have done his work. However, satan, was originally an angel, created by God, to be beautiful, wise and anointed.

> *...This is what the Sovereign LORD says:*
> *"You were the seal of perfection,*
> *full of wisdom and perfect in beauty.*
> *You were in Eden,*
> *the garden of God;*
> *every precious stone adorned you:*
> *carnelian, chrysolite and emerald,*
> *topaz, onyx and jasper,*
> *lapis lazuli,turquoise and beryl.*
> *Your setting and mountings were made of gold;*
> *on the day you were created they were prepared.*
>
> *You were anointed as a guardian cherub,*
> *for so I ordained you.*
> *You were on the holy mount of God;*

you walked among the fiery stones."
Ezekiel 28:12-14 (NIV2011)

This cherub was created to be beautiful and wise. God anointed him to be a trusted guardian cherub. He stood in the very Presence of God. He was awed by God's Power and Majesty. But as time went on, he wanted more. He wanted to know all God knew for one simple purpose. He wanted to be God.

I imagine this cherub practicing day after day to be just like God. He loved the way the rest of the angels worshipped God. He loved the way God could do anything. But try as he might, he was always just one step behind God. He could never quite reach God's Full Heights.

There are references in different books of the Bible that describe satan's fall from Glory.

"You were blameless in your ways
from the day you were created,
till wickedness was found in you.
Through your widespread trade
you were filled with violence,
and you sinned. ..."
Ezekiel 28:15-16 (NIV2011)

What thoughts corrupted one so perfectly created by God?

You said in your heart, "I will ascend to the heavens;
I will raise my throne above the stars of God;
I will sit enthroned on the mount of assembly,
on the utmost heights of Mount Zaphon.
I will ascend above the tops of the clouds;
I will make myself like the Most High."
Isaiah 14:13-14 (NIV2011)

The heart of satan's descent into evil was in his focus. When he began to focus only on himself instead of God, any wisdom he once had became corrupted. He began to make life-changing decisions that would spell doom for him and the followers he gained.

As much as God loves His Creations, He does not withhold judgment. His Rules are the same for all, even disobedient angels.

> *... God did not spare angels when they sinned ...*
> *2 Peter 2:4 (NIV2011)*

> *... "so I drove you in disgrace from the mount of God,*
> *and I expelled you, guardian cherub,*
> *from among the fiery stones.*
> *Your heart became proud*
> *on account of your beauty,*
> *and you corrupted your wisdom*
> *because of your splendor.*
> *So I threw you to the earth;*
> *I made a spectacle of you before kings."*
> *Ezekiel 28:16-17 (NIV2011)*

Chapter 5

God's Grace, Greater Than Any Sin

W hy did God not eliminate satan and anyone who followed him? Couldn't God have stamped out evil and started over? Even when God took some humans off the earth, He never eliminated all of His Creations. God's Plan from the beginning was redemption, not destruction.

> *"I don't want wicked people to die."*
> *declares the Almighty LORD.*
> *"I want them to turn from their evil ways and live."*
> *Ezekiel 18:23 (GW)*

You might say, "Surely God could not love satan." In fact, He does. God continued to talk with satan. He continued to teach satan. God continued to set the boundaries and cast satan out from the places he could not go. But God never eliminated satan.

Satan knows The Word of God. He can quote Scripture. But when he does, he has a variety of ways to try to pull us away from God instead of drawing us to Him.

In spite of satan's bad behavior, God continues to teach him, both through His Word and through His Actions. God Himself lives out what He later spoke through the Words of Jesus.

> *But I say to you, "Love your enemies,*
> *bless those who curse you,*
> *do good to those who hate you,*
> *and pray for those who spitefully use you and persecute you,*
> *that you may be sons of your Father in heaven;*
> *for He makes His sun rise on the evil and on the good,*
> *and sends rain on the just and on the unjust."*
> *Matthew 5:44-45 (NKJV)*

Satan certainly falls in the categories of those who curse God, hate God, attempt to spitefully use God and persecute God. But God continues to love him and withholds nothing from him.

God's Love for His Creations is greater than any sins they commit. God knows how He created us and what He created us to be. When He looks at us, He looks through the pure eyes of Love. His Desire is for us to know how great His Love is.

Nothing, not even our sins, can stop God from loving us.

Paul spoke of God's Great Love, as recorded in Romans.

> *For I am convinced that neither death nor life,*
> *neither angels nor demons,*
> *neither the present nor the future,*
> *nor any powers neither height nor depth,*
> *nor anything else in all creation,*
> *will be able to separate us from the love of God*
> *that is in Christ Jesus our Lord.*
> *Romans 8:38-39 (NIV2011)*

If God could love satan with this kind of love, how could we do less for any other Creation of our Father, even those who have been infected by evil?

However, as much as God loves His Creations, He does not love any evil act. Therefore, He continues to warn us about the actions of His fallen cherub.

Be alert and of sober mind.
Your enemy the devil prowls around like a roaring lion
looking for someone to devour.
Resist him, standing firm in the faith,
because you know that the family of believers throughout the world
is undergoing the same kind of sufferings.
1 Peter 5:8-9 (NIV2011)

Chapter 6

The Knowledge of Good

*T*he Tree from which Adam and Eve were not to eat was an interesting tree. It would give Knowledge of both Good and Evil. Didn't God want them to know Good? Of course! He put them in a world full of things He had pronounced Good. What God did not want Adam and Eve to experience was His Good attached to Evil.

When we recognize all the Good things God has given us, how could we do anything but fall to our knees in thanksgiving and praise?

> *Let us come before him with thanksgiving*
> *and extol him with music and song.*
> *Psalm 95:2 (NIV2011)*

Satan hates our thanking and praising God. Satan sees such contentment as a definite threat to anything he might try to do.

Our giving thanks to God increases the risk we will be satisfied. In thanking God, we realize God alone can provide what we need. Thankfulness is a definite threat to satan.

Satan comes to us as he did to Eve. He presents a scenario that does not deny things might be good now. But he suggests he can improve them. God might give good things, but satan suggests he can do better. Satan entices us to believe he can give us great worldly things. He tried that tactic on Jesus.

Once more the devil took him to a very high mountain
and showed him all the kingdoms in the world and their glory.

The devil said to him,
"I will give you all this if you will bow down and worship me."
Matthew 4:8-9 (GW)

Satan begins weaving the thoughts that God has not provided, but instead, has deprived us of something. If we believe satan can give really great things, then we start to wonder why God just gave us good things.

To understand how great things could be, satan needs to take us shopping. He opens our eyes to the "great things" in life others have. He gives us another bite from the forbidden tree of the Knowledge of Good and Evil. In order to have that extra "good," we might have to do a little evil.

Satan whets our appetite with one of the sins God spoke against in The Ten Commandments. Many sins start with the sin of envy.

"You shall not covet your neighbor's house.
You shall not covet your neighbor's wife,
or his male or female servant,
his ox or donkey,
or anything that belongs to your neighbor."
Exodus 20:17 (NIV2011)

How about his car, his big screen TV, his vacation home, or his cushy job that will let him retire early?

Envy has a way of making us feel the Good we have is not good enough. Envy keeps us striving to have more. If Good is good, would it not follow that more would be better? Within that line of thinking are the seeds that grow into alcoholism, drug addictions, weight problems, and debt.

The other sins God addressed in The Ten Commandments also relate to envy and the desire to have more. If it comes down to it, how do we get more? Satan tempts his victims into lying, stealing, murdering ... even having illicit relationships with another's spouse.

Satan wants to assure we will never be content with what God has given us. He begins with a little whispering that God has deprived us in some way. He then takes us window-shopping to see what everyone else has.

Then satan ices the cake with one direct hit. "Why wait? I can give you what you want right now. Oh sure, God might get around to you one day, but He's busy now. I can serve you right away!"

We live in a world of instants. We don't like to wait. Often we are willing to take something of a lesser quality if we can have it now. Satan does not want us to take enough time to hear The Truth.

> *Wait with hope for the LORD.*
> *Be strong, and let your heart be courageous.*
> *Yes, wait with hope for the LORD.*
> *Psalm 27:14 (GW)*

When satan opens our eyes to the Knowledge of what appears to be Good and then adds the Knowledge of Evil, he is ready to move in for the kill.

Paul talked about the difficult situations he had experienced. However, his need did not drive him to shop with the devil for better times. No, Paul was content, knowing he had the One Thing satan could never give him. Paul had The One,

Who would give him True Strength. Paul knew he was in the Center of God's Love, Protection, and Provision and he planned to stay there.

I am not saying this because I am in need,
for I have learned to be content whatever the circumstances.
I know what it is to be in need, and I know what it is to have plenty.
I have learned the secret of being content in any and every situation,
whether well fed or hungry,
whether living in plenty or in want.
I can do all this through him who gives me strength.
Philippians 4:11-13 (NIV2011)

Jesus dealt with satan's offers speedily. Look what happened when He did.

Jesus said to him,
"Go away, Satan!
Scripture says, 'Worship the Lord your God and serve only him.'"

Then the devil left him, and angels came to take care of him.
Matthew 4:10-11 (GW)

Chapter 7

The Knowledge of Evil

Why would Adam and Eve ever need to know anything about evil? Did it exist? Yes, satan and his demons were already at work before Adam and Eve knew about them. However, their work had not directly affected Adam and Eve.

As long as Adam and Eve did not do business with the evil one, they were unaffected by evil. But everything changed once satan began to play the game of "made you look!"

We begin to learn about evil from the beginning of our lives. We want our children to recognize evil, so they will stay away from it. As we grow, we learn more and more about evil. Finally we are adults, watching the bad news of evil around the world. Is it possible that in our desire to keep evil at bay, we only perpetuate it?

Instead of spreading the Good News of God's Grace, Mercy, and Provision, we spread the bad news of what appear to be triumphs for satan. Every time something bad happens, satan is quick to rush in and question, "Where was your God in this one?"

Many things we perceive as tragedies have been called "Acts of God." Sadly, the wondrous miracles God does on a regular basis are not attributed to Him. Because of this double standard, fear and doubt begin to creep into our thoughts.

We begin to think of all the bad things that have happened to others or ourselves. We think of all the times we have prayed that God would fix things the way we felt they should be fixed. And He didn't.

Satan does not want us to think very long about evil being associated with him. This is one place he is willing to throw the ball to God. He is quick to point out that if God is indeed all-powerful, then He could have rescued His People. Even better, He could have prevented any problems from the beginning.

After satan is through with thoroughly trashing God, his next move is to say, "You see how it is. You're really alone in this world. So you need to be better prepared next time to deal with evil. You need to know all about how it works. Fortunately I can help you. Let me show you what evil looks like."

Once satan convinces us we need to know about evil, he has us hooked. He has a variety of tricks up his sleeve to keep us looking through his bags of evil. But we will discover, as did Adam and Eve, that it will be impossible to put evil back in the bag. How does satan hook us?

Many people are lured in by the "everybody's doing it" temptation. If "everybody is doing it," how could it be that bad? Sometimes we just want to belong. If we do what everyone else is doing, it makes us part of a club, so to speak. We long to belong.

Sometimes we have the feeling of "don't go there" and yet we do go there. We tell ourselves we can always turn around and stop, if it really turns out to be that bad. Yet, after we are on the roller coaster ride of whatever both terrifies and excites us, we find ourselves drawn to it again and again.

Knowledge of evil, pain, and suffering is a terrible burden. Satan attempts to drag us back to a past full of regrets. Then he throws us into his scary peek into the future.

Many people spend endless hours of torment with the thoughts of what they or others have experienced in the clutches of evil. Often the result of sin is an all encompassing regret that results in our believing God will never forgive us. If God will never forgive us, then our first urge is not to run to God, but to run away from God. And where can we go, when our past, present and future all seem terrifying?

So are we doomed to a life of darkness because we got taken in by satan? No. In just nine words, James gave us a Lasting Truth about satan, aka the devil.

> *Resist the devil, and he will flee from you.*
> *James 4:7 (NIV2011)*

When there is so much bad all around us, isn't the "cat already out of the bag," so to speak? Many people attempt to conquer evil by pushing back against it and shooting or clubbing it to death. Some actually go looking for evil, in an effort to cast out every demon they can find.

Satan laughs, as they exhaust themselves in a hunt that never ends. The more they devote themselves to the elimination of evil, the less time they have to spread God's Good.

Jesus told us about the principle of Light and Darkness.

> *Jesus spoke to the Pharisees again.*
> *He said, "I am the light of the world.*
> *Whoever follows me will have a life filled with light*
> *and will never live in the dark."*
> *John 8:12 (GW)*

The light shines in the dark,
and the dark has never extinguished it.
John 1:5 (GW)

Both John and Paul, as recorded in the New Testament, echo the way to defeat satan.

This is the message we heard from Christ and are reporting to you:
God is light, and there isn't any darkness in him.
If we say, "We have a relationship with God"
and yet live in the dark, we're lying.
We aren't being truthful.
But if we live in the light in the same way that God is in the light,
we have a relationship with each other.
And the blood of his Son Jesus cleanses us from every sin.
1 John 1:5-7 (GW)

The Truth is we have a choice. Even if we have messed up and chosen satan's way, we can stop and turn around. We will find Jesus waiting, with all The Power to purify us of all sin.

What if satan comes back and tries to offer us our sins back? Don't listen to him. Thank God you don't live in satan's camp anymore. Don't doubt! You made the right choice. Now keep making the right choices.

Never worry about anything.
But in every situation let God know what you need
in prayers and requests while giving thanks.
Then God's peace, which goes beyond anything we can imagine,
will guard your thoughts and emotions through Christ Jesus.

Finally, brothers and sisters,
keep your thoughts on whatever is right or deserves praise:

things that are true, honorable, fair,
pure, acceptable, or commendable.
Practice what you've learned and received from me,
what you heard and saw me do.
Then the God who gives this peace will be with you.
Philippians 4:6-9 (GW)

Don't miss the point Adam and Eve were about to miss. It is our privilege to make a choice for Good. However, we cannot create Good by ourselves. The battle of Good and Evil started long before we were ever aware of it. The Creator of The Light is the only One Who can eliminate the darkness.

"...Do not be afraid or discouraged because of this vast army.
For the battle is not yours, but God's."
2 Chronicles 20:15 (NIV2011)

Chapter 8

Is Knowledge Power?

Humans were created with the ability to make a choice. Satan could not snatch God's children out of His Hands. Satan could only entice them to use their gift of free choice to choose him. Satan had to appear to offer a better deal than God.

What could satan possibly offer that would draw Adam and Eve to choose anything other than the heaven God had already given them?

Satan got them to buy into one false premise that still circulates today. That false premise is "Knowledge is Power!"

How many times have we asked God to explain something and He was silent? How many times have we asked God to follow what we were sure was the right course of action and He did not do what we asked?

Does the thought ever come to mind that if you just knew everything God knew, you could either take care of things yourself or at least you might understand better why God is doing or not doing what He does?

... the snake told the woman.
"God knows that when you eat it
[the fruit of the tree of the knowledge of good and evil],
your eyes will be opened.
You'll be like God, knowing good and evil."
Genesis 3:4-5 (GW)

Would that get your attention? What if you knew you could know everything God knows? And, further, how would it make you feel to know that God doesn't want you to know all He knows?

Why did Eve eat the fruit satan offered her?

The woman saw that the tree had fruit that was good to eat,
nice to look at, and desirable for making someone wise.
So she took some of the fruit and ate it. ...
Genesis 3:6 (GW)

What was there about the forbidden fruit that tempted Eve?

It was good for food. Eve already had all the delicious food she would ever need.

It was pleasing to the eye. Eve already had a garden full of things that were pleasing to her eyes.

It was desirable for gaining wisdom. Eve suddenly believed perhaps she did not have wisdom. Eve wanted to know all God knew. If God truly loved her, wouldn't He have given her the right to know all He knew? Satan had been able to place a small wedge of doubt about God's Love and Provision.

Eve did remember what God had told her.

"But you must never eat from the tree of the knowledge of good and evil because when you eat from it, you will certainly die."
Genesis 2:17 (GW)

What was dying? Eve did not know. She obviously did not have all knowledge. Have you ever been lured into something evil by the thought you could make a better choice about whether it was bad, if you could just experience it once?

Eve did not stop and ask God to answer her questions. She listened to satan. She believed he could give her instant access to the special knowledge to which she was entitled. Eve did not recognize the Gifts God had already given her. She believed the outright lies of satan. She made a choice to disobey God. In so doing, Eve set into motion the wheels of a great disaster.

Chapter 9

What You Know or WHO You Know?

D oes God want to keep secrets from us? Didn't He say His Ways are not our ways? He did say that.

> *"For my thoughts are not your thoughts,*
> *neither are your ways my ways,"*
> *declares The LORD.*

> *"As the heavens are higher than the earth,*
> *so are my ways higher than your ways*
> *and my thoughts than your thoughts."*
> *Isaiah 55:8-9 (NIV2011)*

So should we give up? No! Listen to what David, the one who was characterized as a man after God's own heart, said. He approached God in humility and asked God to teach him.

> *Show me your ways, LORD,*
> *teach me your paths.*
> *Guide me in your truth and teach me,*
> *for you are God my Savior,*

and my hope is in you all day long.
Psalm 25:4-5 (NIV2011)

Since God said so plainly His Ways are not our ways, doesn't it sound a little daring to think of asking God to show us His Ways? James assured us God would not mind our questions.

If any of you needs wisdom to know what you should do, you should ask God,
and he will give it to you.
God is generous to everyone and doesn't find fault with them.
James 1:5 (GW)

God wants us to know His Ways, Ways that are so far above what we can even think or imagine, that they are "unsearchable." Some things you will never find in books or on the Internet. Some knowledge will only come to you directly from God.

Call to me, and I will answer you.
I will tell you great and mysterious things
that you do not know.
Jeremiah 33:3 (GW)

But, in order to learn about God's Ways, we will have to learn first about God … The One Who knows us completely and loves us completely, as no other will ever be able to do.

God calls to us, as in the game of hide and seek. As we search for Him, we will discover untold treasures everywhere we look.

You will seek me and find me
when you seek me with all your heart.
Jeremiah 29:13 (NIV2011)

Chapter 10

Where Are You?

Sometimes when we are in the act of sinning, we actually do not recognize that what we are doing is sin. Or we may know we are doing something that is a "little shady," but, we think it's not that bad, by the world's standards.

When we measure our actions against those of other humans, it is easy to say, "Hey, I'm not that bad."

But when God shines the full Light of Himself on us, and we measure ourselves against the Standards of God, we can quickly see how far we have fallen.

Our first urge is not to run to God, but instead, to run away and hide. That is exactly what Adam and Eve did. After they ate the forbidden fruit, their eyes were open and they realized they were uncovered, exposed, and unprotected.

They not only saw evil for the first time, but they also began to experience the feelings that were consequences of evil. They felt fear. They felt shame. They felt panic in trying to cover their nakedness. They did what we often do. They tried to cover their outsides to hide the wickedness of what had crept inside them. They sewed fig leaves together and tried to cover themselves.

Then the man and his wife heard the sound of the LORD God
as he was walking in the garden in the cool of the day,
and they hid from the LORD God among the trees of the garden.
Genesis 3:8 (NIV2011)

God had been with Adam and Eve all along. But, when they began to listen to the voice of satan, they no longer heard God. Now, they heard Him clearly. The Lord asked them one pivotal question.

… "Where are you?"
Genesis 3:9 (GW)

Take a few moments right now and hear God asking you that question. Where are you in this life? Where are you in your relationship with God, your Creator?

Are there forbidden fruits you have sampled? Are there paths you have chosen that led to places you never intended to go? Have you been in hiding from God, fearing the day would come when He would find you?

Have you tried very hard to find the right things that would cover you? Have you tried desperately to cover past sins with good actions today? Have you discovered that no matter how many good acts you do, you can't keep covered all you want to keep covered? Are you running out of fig leaves?

God is not yelling. He is close enough to whisper, "Where are you?"

Chapter 11

Busted!

*A*dam answered God honestly.

> *He answered,*
> *"I heard you in the garden.*
> *I was afraid because I was naked,*
> *so I hid."*
> *Genesis 3:10 (GW)*

Ever been there? When we discover we are in a real mess, we go directly to our thoughts and feelings, with no real consideration of how we got there. We may finally sense we are in a bad place and we are afraid. We agree to talk to God because we really want Him to fix things. "Dear God, please get me out of this mess!"

But God does not want to condemn us or punish us. He does not want to just do a quick rescue and be on His Way. He wants us to learn lessons that will help keep us out of trouble in the future. God wants to teach us. He wants us to understand how we came to be where we are, in the hopes we will learn not to go there again.

God asked Adam two questions.

> *God asked,*
> *"Who told you that you were naked?*
> *Did you eat fruit from the tree I commanded you not to eat from?"*
> *Genesis 3:11 (GW)*

What followed was a series of finger pointings by both Adam and Eve. Adam pointed out that God had given him the woman and she had done this thing. Eve pointed to the serpent, and correctly identified she had been deceived.

God did not bother to ask the serpent why he had done what he had done. He knew why each had done what they had done. But God knew satan would never own up to his part.

So now what? The two humans were standing there with a pathetic half covering of fig leaves. And the serpent was standing there, probably smiling. (And yes, the serpent was probably still standing at that time.)

We may believe that recognizing we made bad choices and repenting is enough to reset things to where they were before. The Truth is God wants us to be in a better place than we were before the crisis happened. Even if we wanted to, we can never go back. We can be forgiven, but there are still consequences of any actions we have taken.

> *Do not reject the discipline of the LORD, my son,*
> *and do not resent his warning,*
> *because the LORD warns the one he loves,*
> *even as a father warns a son with whom he is pleased.*
> *Proverbs 3:11-12 (GW)*

God loved His Children. His Desire was not for punishment, but for discipline, to teach them again about boundaries and the importance of staying within His Love. His Message to them was the same as is His Message to us.

As recorded in the Gospel of John, Chapter 15, Jesus gave the same directive multiple times. (Underlines added for emphasis)

"<u>Remain in me, as I also remain in you.</u>
No branch can bear fruit by itself; it must remain in the vine.
Neither can you bear fruit unless <u>you remain in me.</u>"
John 15:4 (NIV2011)

" ...If <u>you remain in me</u> and I in you, you will bear much fruit;
apart from me you can do nothing.
If you do not <u>remain in me</u>,
you are like a branch that is thrown away and withers;
such branches are picked up, thrown into the fire and burned.
If you <u>remain in me and my words remain in you</u>,
ask whatever you wish, and it will be done for you."
John 15:5-7 (NIV2011)

"As the Father has loved me, so have I loved you.
Now <u>remain in my love.</u>
If you keep my commands, you will <u>remain in my love</u>,
just as I have kept my Father's commands
and <u>remain in his love</u>."
John 15:9-10 (NIV2011)

Chapter 12

Discipline versus Punishment

*T*he dictionary defines the word, discipline, as "training to act in accordance with rules."[1]

There is a difference in discipline and punishment. Many see what happened next in the story of Adam and Eve to be severe punishment inflicted by God. It then becomes easy to see God through this lens of harsh judgment all the way through the Bible.

Much of the Easter story, as interpreted by some, centers around an angry God, Who hated our sin so much He wanted to beat the tar out of us and then kill us. That is terrifying in itself!

But even more disturbing is what appears to be have been God's Solution. If we are to believe what we are often taught, then we would believe instead of beating the stuffings out of us and then killing us, God pinned all of our sins on His Son. Then God did to Him what He really wanted to do to us.

Popular movies and tv presentations leave us quaking in our boots, after watching scenes of unimaginable violence. Anyone who had truly abusive parents remember their lives under the rule of terror. It becomes all too easy for satan to convince us that God is an abusive parent. Many accept Jesus, not out of Love, but out of a desperate attempt to appease what they believe is an angry God.

Many religions believed their gods were to be feared and appeased. If something went wrong in their lives, they were convinced the gods had turned against them because of something they did. They felt they had to quickly do something to get back on their good side or they would be ferociously punished.

Our God is different. He is gentle and humble. He wants to be linked to us in one yoke, so we can learn from Him, up close and personal. He wants to walk right next to us and keep His eyes fixed on us in Love.

> *The LORD is compassionate, merciful, patient,*
> *and always ready to forgive.*
> *Psalm 103:8 (GW)*

> *"Come to Me, all who are weary and heavy-laden,*
> *and I will give you rest.*
> *"Take My yoke upon you and learn from Me,*
> *for I am gentle and humble in heart,*
> *and YOU WILL FIND REST FOR YOUR SOULS."*
> *Matthew 11:28-29 (NASB)*

> *I will instruct you and teach you in the way you should go;*
> *I will counsel you with my loving eye on you.*
> *Psalm 32:8 (NIV2011)*

Our God takes no delight in the death of the wicked. Instead He wants them to turn from their wicked ways and enjoy Life.

> *"Tell them, 'As I live, declares the Almighty LORD,*
> *I don't want wicked people to die.*
> *Rather, I want them to turn from their ways and live.*

Change the way you think and act!
Turn from your wicked ways! …'"
Ezekiel 33:11 (GW)

Could God have wiped out satan, the rebellious angels, Adam and Eve and just started over? Yes, He could have. But if He had done so, it would have meant we are all expendable. If we turned out less than God's Perfect Design for us, He could waste us.

But He does not do that. He disciplines us in love. He seeks disciples. He does not condemn. He saves and redeems us!

For God did not send his Son into the world to condemn the world,
but to save the world through him.
John 3:17 (NIV2011)

So how could God deal with this mess of disobedience from Adam and Eve? How could God wipe the smile off of satan's face?

God, being the Creative God and Father He is, knew exactly how to get Adam and Eve to remain in His Love. He made them junior partners in Creation!

1. Dictionary.com. Dictionary.com, LLC, Web. 6 June 2015. <dictionary.reference.com/browse/discipline>

Chapter 13

A New Position for Satan

*F*irst God dealt with satan.

> *So the LORD God said to the snake,*
> *"Because you have done this,*
> *You are cursed more than all the wild or domestic animals.*
> *You will crawl on your belly.*
> *You will be the lowest of animals as long as you live.*
> *I will make you and the woman hostile toward each other.*
> *I will make your descendants and her descendant hostile toward each other.*
> *He will crush your head, and you will bruise his heel."*
> *Genesis 3:14-15 (GW)*

The dust of the ground was what God used to create Adam. The dust of the ground formed the foundation of God's Earth. It was His to command. It was not satan's. God put satan in a low position of forced humility, far below the heights to which he had once aspired.

He would look at the ground every day and realize he could not create one thing out of it. He was not God.

The livestock and other wild animals would look down on satan, not up, as he had envisioned.

The man and woman would look down to the roots of their creation also, and when they saw the serpent, they would be reminded of how much even a brief association with him had cost them. They would be enemies. Even when satan would try to get their attention by striking at their feet, they would crush him. They could keep crushing him, but they could never kill him. God alone was in charge of satan's life and death.

Was this God's act of revenge on satan? No. It was an act of discipline. God continued to teach satan. Would there ever be any way satan could get off the ground? Yes, but it was not a way he was likely to choose.

> *Humble yourselves before the Lord,*
> *and he will lift you up.*
> *James 4:10 (NIV2011)*

Chapter 14

Motherhood — Partnering With God in Creation

od then turned to Eve. Eve had chosen the way of disobedience. She had decided not all of God's Laws applied to her. She had believed she could control her destiny, if only she were as wise as God.

Eve had not yet recognized her Oneness with God, her Creator. Eve had not yet experienced a true Oneness with her husband.

Eve had not yet learned about a kind of Love that would desire Life so much it would accept pain to produce it. She had not yet experienced a Force inside of her that was so great she would have to submit to it in order to bring Life into the world.

Eve would experience through her own body what it was like for a human to abide within the protection of a womb. She would have nine months to ponder how this tiny human seemed to have everything he needed, while staying within the bounds God had set inside of her.

And yes, even amid the wonder and joy, Eve would feel pain, as she participated in the delivery of that life into the world. She would have a small taste of suffering in comparison to the suffering of Jesus. But, she, like Jesus, would be willing to endure the pain for the Joy of New Life to come through her body.

(Spoken of Jesus)
…He saw the joy ahead of him, so he endured death on the cross…
Hebrews 12:2 (GW)

But rejoice inasmuch as you participate in the sufferings of Christ,
so that you may be overjoyed when his glory is revealed.
1 Peter 4:13 (NIV2011)

As great as had been her sin, God was still to honor Eve by allowing her to participate in suffering to bring Life. God allowed Eve to be the first mother on earth.

He said to the woman,
"I will increase your pain and your labor
when you give birth to children.
Yet, you will long for your husband, and he will rule you."
Genesis 3:16 (GW)

Eve would learn a valuable lesson about submission. Submission to one who loves you is much better than submitting to one who does not love you.

Submit yourselves, then, to God.
Resist the devil, and he will flee from you.
James 4:7 (NIV2011)

In the submission to God and to her husband, Eve found something more beautiful and satisfying than anything she had seen in the Garden. She learned the Joy of God allowing her to partner with Him in creation!

Adam made love to his wife Eve,
and she became pregnant and gave birth to Cain.
She said,
"With the help of the LORD I have brought forth a man."
Genesis 4:1 (NIV2011)

Chapter 15

Farming — Partnering with God in Creation

*A*dam had sinned in several ways. Like Eve, he disobeyed God. He chose the way of wanting more wisdom than he felt God had given or would give him.

Why would he do this? While his reasons may have been similar to those of Eve, it is also possible he did not want to chance Eve having more wisdom than he. This kind of competition resulting from the sin of pride would be carried down to Adam's sons, as they competed for approval.

But Adam fell even further than Eve, when he attempted to outright blame God for his sins. Let's go back and look again at what Adam had to say about why he ate the forbidden fruit.

> *The man answered,*
> *"That woman, the one you gave me,*
> *gave me some fruit from the tree, and I ate it."*
> *Genesis 3:12 (GW)*

How easy it is to blame our sin on God. "Well, God, You made me this way. I can't do any better. It's really not my fault."

"Well, God, if You had not wanted me to do this, You would not have allowed this temptation to be put in my path."

"God, if You wanted me to stop, You know You could have stopped me."

"God, You gave me the gun and held my hand while I pulled the trigger. I thought it was ok with You."

Adam took no responsibilities for his own actions or those of his wife. And he failed to carry out his assignment of caring for the garden in which God placed him. Remember that was Adam's job.

Then the LORD God took the man
and put him in the Garden of Eden
to farm the land and to take care of it.
Genesis 2:15 (GW)

And now God turned to Adam and revealed what was to be his rehabilitation program.

" ... The ground is cursed because of you.
Through hard work you will eat {food that comes} from it
every day of your life.

The ground will grow thorns and thistles for you,
and you will eat wild plants.
By the sweat of your brow,
you will produce food to eat
until you return to the ground,
because you were taken from it.
You are dust,
and you will return to dust."
Genesis 3:17-19 (GW)

Note: God did not curse Adam. He simply changed the process of how easily Adam's food would come from the ground. No more free rides! Adam would have to work for his food.

He would be constantly reminded of the dust from which he came and the dust to which his body would return. He would be reminded daily that the dirt without life in it was just dirt. But with the Power of God in that ground, amazing things would happen.

Adam would plant seeds that looked like nothing. He would tend and water the seeds. He would pull the weeds away from his plants. He would leave the plants in the ground for just the right amount of time and then he would appreciate the harvest that came forth. But Adam would know, that, as much as he had been allowed to be a partner in creation, he was just that—a partner. Only God could cause the Life in that soil to spring forth. God alone was God.

Adam would also look at the thorns and thistles that grew among his plants. They were sharp and pricked his fingers. As Adam watched drops of blood trickle from his fingers, he would be reminded again that life was fragile and needed to be guarded.

Adam would also see the serpent from time to time in his garden. The serpent would hiss and try to strike Adam, but Adam quickly subdued Him. The serpent crawled away among the thorns and thistles, dreaming of another day when he, like the thorns, would be lifted up in full view of all.

But it was not satan who would wear a crown, even one of thorns. It would be Jesus. Satan thought that future day would be his victory day. It would not. It would be a time when God would allow satan to be lifted up just long enough to expose him, and then he would be cast even lower than the ground on which he now crawled.

Adam found something more in his rehabilitation. He too was a partner in bringing life into the world. The food provided by God and tended and harvested by Adam was not just for himself. Adam, like Eve, was able, with God, to bring life to a new generation of people by his becoming one with God, one with his wife and remaining faithful to what God had called Him to do.

Adam never forgot again who was in charge and who really knew all anyone needed to know. As Adam labored, he knew he was not alone. The Master Gardener labored along side of him.

"I am the true vine, and my Father is the gardener."
John 15:1 (NIV2011)

Chapter 16

Uncovered and Exposed

*A*dam and Eve had tried to cover themselves. When they opened the door to the knowledge of evil, they felt every feeling and sensation that went with evil. They felt the effects of cold and heat. They felt pain. They felt sorrow and regret. They felt fear. They felt shame.

When they realized their exposure to this new world, they tried to cover themselves. But the fig leaves they used only partially covered them. Satan likely influenced their choice of what to cover. Some translations of the Bible indicate they made loincloths, thus covering the parts of their bodies that would be used to perpetuate life on earth.

> *Then the eyes of both of them were opened,*
> *and they knew that they were naked;*
> *and they sewed fig leaves together*
> *and made themselves loin coverings.*
> *Genesis 3:7 (NASB)*

Satan did not want this life to be perpetuated, unless he could control it. Satan may have felt if he could only have just Adam and Eve under his spell long enough for them to eat of the Tree of Life, it would be enough. They would live forever, and satan could continue to influence them.

Satan had many things in mind they could do with their intimate parts. For satan, it was essential that Adam and Eve never realize why God had created their bodies in such a unique way. Satan had already begun to separate them in their sin and blaming of each other. It was his express mission that they never realize who they were in unity with God and with each other.

God had done something unique from the beginning that would assure He would always be a part of His Living Creatures. He would always be as close to them as their very breath.

Chapter 17

The Kiss of God

*H*ow were Adam and Eve created? Let's back up and review.

Then the LORD God formed man
of dust from the ground,
and breathed into his nostrils
the breath of life;
and man became a living being.
Genesis 2:7 (NASB)

God is the Master Creator. God took the dust of the ground and shaped and formed it into a man. Then God breathed His Breath into Adam's nostrils.

God was face to face with His Creation. Just as humans learn to show intimate affection by kissing, and being close enough to share breaths, God set the example from the beginning.

What was the significance of God's Breath? He was sharing His Very Self with His human creations. He was placing within each of us The Power of His Holy Spirit! He was assuring He and His Creation would never be apart!

The Spirit of God was in full operation long before Jesus was visible in human form. David the Psalmist rightly observed,

> *By the word of the LORD the heavens were made,*
> *And by the breath of His mouth all their host.*
> *Psalm 33:6 (NASB)*

Job's friend, Elihu rightly observed,

> *"God's Spirit has made me.*
> *The breath of the Almighty gives me life."*
> *Job 33:4 (GW)*

God put Himself inside of all of His Creations from their first breath. Whether we have ever recognized it or not, we are joined with Him. David the Psalmist was awed by his discovery of how much he was joined at every moment to God's Spirit within him.

> *Where can I go to get away from your Spirit?*
> *Where can I run to get away from you?*
> *If I go up to heaven, you are there.*
> *If I make my bed in hell, you are there.*
> *If I climb upward on the rays of the morning sun*
> *or land on the most distant shore of the sea where the sun sets,*
> *even there your hand would guide me*
> *and your right hand would hold on to me.*
> *Psalm 139:7-10 (GW)*

Paul made the same discovery.

> *I am convinced that nothing can ever separate us from God's love*
> *which Christ Jesus our Lord shows us.*
> *We can't be separated by death or life, by angels or rulers,*
> *by anything in the present or anything in the future,*

> *by forces or powers in the world above or in the world below,*
> *or by anything else in creation.*
> Romans 8:38-39 (GW)

At the time of physical death, The Spirit returns to God. The physical body left on earth has served its purpose well, but the Life that was inside it has left that place of confinement. It has moved up into a new, even more glorious Union with God.

> *then the dust will return to the earth as it was,*
> *and the spirit will return to God who gave it.*
> Ecclesiastes 12:7 (NASB)

God begins our Life with a variation of what we know as a kiss. God blew into our bodies His Holy Spirit through His Breath. Perhaps He ends our earthly life by another Kiss, in which we joyfully release His Spirit back unto Him.

It may be a new concept to consider that God's Holy Spirit was in us from the beginning and ever shall be. Sometimes it feels we are more in control if we can give a date on which we "invited Jesus in" and then another date in time on which we "received The Holy Spirit."

However, it is more accurate to say that at some point in time, we discovered He Who was in us all along. We begin to see external evidence of what was internal.

"Wait!" you may say. "I know plenty of people who show no evidence of The Holy Spirit living inside of them. It seems to be the spirit of satan who is driving them. Where is The Spirit of God?"

A house may be completely wired for electricity, but if we do not flip the switch to turn on the light, it will be dark. It will be easy to become confused, fearful and angry, as we try to find our way in the dark.

Jesus spoke of the condition of those who do not acknowledge The Light within them.

"The eye is the lamp of the body.
So if your eye is unclouded, your whole body will be full of light.
But if your eye is evil,
your whole body will be full of darkness.
If the light in you is darkness, how dark it will be!"
Matthew 6:22-23 (GW)

We were created from the beginning to know we are Children of The Light. We were created pure in heart. We came from The Light Himself, Who stays within us. However, living in a world contaminated with all manner of sin quickly causes us to forget who we are.

It would be as if we were created perfectly clean, but quickly became dirty, as we tried to negotiate a world full of mud puddles. But God's Spirit continues to call to us from the Heavens, from the earth around us, and from within us.

Once we become aware there is something more than a world of mud, we then have to desire to have Light, and not darkness. Once we remember who we are and discover that He Who made us is still creating us, we have a choice.

We can continue to hide in the darkness, afraid of what His Light will reveal about us. Or we can allow The One Who already sees through our darkness to turn on The Light.

Jesus said to them again,
"Peace be with you!
As The Father has sent me,
I am sending you."

After he had said this,
he breathed on the disciples and said,

71

"Receive the Holy Spirit."
John 20:21-22 (GW)

The One will reveal more and more of His Light, as we are willing to receive more from Him. And we can anticipate that day when God will throw back the covers from this earthly body and reveal fully His Spirit. We will remember our first kiss from Him that started our earthly life.

In that moment of Great Joy, we will see Him once again, Face to Face!

... then we shall see face to face.
Now I know in part;
then I shall know fully, even as I am fully known.
1 Corinthians 13:12 (NIV2011)

Chapter 18

I'll Be Near Your Heart!

*G*od not only joined Himself with Adam and Eve, but He also joined them to each other. He did so in a most creative way. God created Eve, in part, from Adam.

So the LORD God caused him to fall into a deep sleep.
While the man was sleeping,
the LORD God took out one of the man's ribs
and closed up the flesh at that place.
Then the LORD God formed a woman from the rib
that he had taken from the man.
He brought her to the man.

The man said,
"This is now bone of my bones
and flesh of my flesh.
She will be named woman
because she was taken from man."

That is why a man will leave his father and mother
and will be united with his wife,
and they will become one flesh.
Genesis 2:21-24 (GW)

God linked Adam and Eve together. Perhaps Adam would always have the sense of longing for the one who was made from a part of his own body. He would see Eve and know they shared something more than what anyone could see on the surface. Adam would have a sense of needing Eve in a physical way to complete him. Eve would desire her husband, sensing she carried a part of him in her body.

The desire of a husband and wife to be physically connected was a part of God's Plan. Adam and Eve would discover how God had creatively provided a way for them to physically come together.

But before we discuss the ultimate Celebration of Oneness, let's go back to God's selection of Adam's rib. Why would God choose a rib from Adam to give to Eve?

The human body is a magnificent Creation of God, perfectly designed to be our "mobile home" while we live on earth. Each part of the body fulfills multiple functions. Each part of the body works in both unity and harmony with the other parts of the body. Additionally, they all work together in perfect timing.

When David the Psalmist considered God's Creation of his body, he was awed.

> *You alone created my inner being.*
> *You knitted me together inside my mother.*
> *I will give thanks to you because*
> *I have been so amazingly and miraculously made.*
> *Your works are miraculous,*
> *and my soul is fully aware of this.*
> *Psalm 139:13-14 (GW)*

Let's look at one part of that amazing body—the ribs.

The ribs provide protection for the lungs and heart. They curl around these organs like a shield.

Ribs are one of the few bones that continue to make red marrow (and thus red blood cells) in the adult. The red blood cells carry oxygen to all parts of the body.

Ribs serve as attachment points for chest muscles involved in breathing.

Think of it. God provided ribs for protection, continued production of the red blood cells that carry oxygen to the body, and as an important part of the act of breathing and providing oxygen to the blood cells.

We have already seen how God provided His Breath as the important Power to keep His human creations functioning. Now God brought Adam and Eve into a special shared relationship by using one of the bones that are vital to breathing.

Ribs are amazing in yet another way. Although all bones can repair themselves, ribs can regenerate themselves. Ribs are commonly removed during surgeries that require bone grafts in other parts of the body.[1]

God chose from Adam a bone that could regenerate itself!

God also spoke to Eve's relationship to Adam through His Selection of a rib. Matthew Henry, from his review of Genesis 2:21-25, stated, "That the woman was made of a rib out of the side of Adam; not made out of his head to rule over him, nor out of his feet to be trampled upon by him, but out of his side to be equal with him, under his arm to be protected, and near his heart to be beloved."

1. Moore, K.L. and Dailey, A.F., Clinically Oriented Anatomy, 4th ed. Philadelphia: Lippincott Williams & Wilkins, 1999. Print.

Chapter 19

Holy Oneness

$\mathcal{A}$ dam and Eve did desire to be one. It was not just about a rib. They wanted to be connected in Love. It was a Holy Desire that seemed to come from the inside of them.

They discovered their hands were similar. At first they just touched. Then they discovered their fingers could intertwine with each other. They could walk together, holding hands, their bodies joined in part.

They discovered they could extend their arms around each other's bodies in a hug that brought their hearts close to each other. They did not understand why, but it felt good and right. Perhaps it was the feeling that the rib of Adam, now the rib of Eve, was back close to where God had originally created it.

Adam and Eve had been so busy looking at everything in the garden they had not really looked at each other. Now they did. They saw how different they were, but they also saw how alike they were. They looked at each other, face to face.

As they came closer to each other in a holy hug, they could feel not only the beating of each other's hearts, but they could also feel the breath from the other on their face. Their breaths began to synch with each other. Then they put their lips together in the first holy kiss.

All of this was designed by God as a visible picture of what He wants our relationship with Him to be. He wants to touch us. He wants to be inside of us, connected as a Beautiful One.

God believes in total commitment. He is completely committed to us. He wants us to be completely committed to Him. His Love for us is everlasting. He uses Words that express unchanging and complete Love.

> " …*I have loved you with an everlasting love …*"
> *Jeremiah 31:3 (NIV2011)*

> "…*Never will I leave you;*
> *never will I forsake you.*"
> *Hebrews 13:5 (NIV2011)*

> "…*I am with you always …*"
> *Matthew 28:20 (NIV2011)*

God intended that Adam and Eve and all couples who would follow them would be committed to Him and to each other. Jesus spoke of True Love, as God intended it.

> "*But God made them male and female in the beginning, at creation.*
> *That's why a man will leave his father and mother*
> *and will remain united with his wife,*
> *and the two will be one. So they are no longer two but one.*
> *Therefore, don't let anyone separate what God has joined together.*"
> *Mark 10:6-9 (GW)*

God's Creative Design for Oneness was not limited to touch, hand holding, hugging or even the kiss of True Love. God is already physically united with us. God wants to be One with us—completely joined in One Heart, Soul and Spirit.

The ultimate Celebration of True Love is to be together completely. Jesus wanted His Followers to understand what truly being One with Him would mean.

Where does True Love of the Lord lead? And how is that True Love demonstrated through the bodies of humans?

> *"On that day you will realize that I am in my Father,*
> *and you are in me,*
> *and I am in you."*
> *John 14:20 (NIV2011)*

In True Love, the moment comes when we must consider whether we can trust the one we love to move from the outside of us to the inside of us.

As much as God enjoys being with us on any level, what He desires is the most intimate of all relationships. He wants us to be willing to be completely uncovered and honest before Him, and He wants to reveal Himself to us. God offers us all of His Love. He will not force Himself on us. He waits for us to accept His Love.

There was a day when David the Psalmist discovered The Glory of The Lord in a new place. He was awed. He saw The Glory of The Lord inside of himself!

Let's join David, as he considered what it meant to be known by the One, Who knew him completely.

Chapter 20

Oh God, You Know Me!

You have searched me, LORD,
and you know me.
You know when I sit and when I rise;
you perceive my thoughts from afar.
You discern my going out and my lying down;
you are familiar with all my ways.
Before a word is on my tongue
you, LORD, know it completely.
You hem me in behind and before,
and you lay your hand upon me.
Such knowledge is too wonderful for me,
too lofty for me to attain.

Where can I go from your Spirit?
Where can I flee from your presence?
If I go up to the heavens, you are there;
If I make my bed in the depths, you are there.
If I rise on the wings of the dawn,
if I settle on the far side of the sea,
even there your hand will guide me,
your right hand will hold me fast.
If I say, "Surely the darkness will hide me
and the light become night around me,"
even the darkness will not be dark to you;
the night will shine like the day,
for darkness is as light to you.

For you created my inmost being;
you knit me together in my mother's womb.
I praise you because I am fearfully and wonderfully made;
your works are wonderful,
I know that full well.
My frame was not hidden from you
when I was made in the secret place,
when I was woven together in the depths of the earth.
Your eyes saw my unformed body;
all the days ordained for me were written in your book
before one of them came to be.

How precious to me are your thoughts, God!
How vast is the sum of them!
Were I to count them,
they would outnumber the grains of sand—
when I awake, I am still with you.
Psalm 139:1-18 (NIV2011)

If God has such complete knowledge of us, we might wonder why He would want to be One with us. One lingering question always seems to creep into any potential relationship. "If you really knew me, would you still love me?"

Often when we get close to an intimate, committed relationship, we hesitate. It is not that we do not love our Beloved. We do love him. But we cannot believe our Beloved would love us, if He really knew us. The fear of rejection is one of satan's greatest tools to keep us from having a deep relationship with God.

When you look in your mirror, do you see the same beautiful person God sees?

Chapter 21

Who Am I?

*A*fter taking that bite of forbidden fruit, Adam and Eve experienced feelings they had never felt before. Satan's leading weapon for condemning us is his use of shame.

In order for shame to be effective, we have to have both knowledge of Good and Evil. Satan is a deceiver. We start out sure of what we know. Satan casts doubt on whether we really understood. Then he switches things so quickly we never notice. God is Good. Satan is Evil. However, if satan were to allow us to see the Truth, he would be defeated on the spot.

So, he quickly attempts to change our view. He tries to get us to believe we are the evil ones. He tells us we have fallen so far God would want nothing to do with us now, except to punish us severely. That is a lie. Remember who satan really is.

> " ... *When he lies, he speaks his native language,*
> *for he is a liar and the father of lies.*"
> *John 8: 44 (NIV2011)*

" ... the accuser of our brothers and sisters,
who accuses them before our God day and night ..."
Revelation 12:10 (NIV2011)

When we see ourselves as evil beyond the reach of God's Grace, it is likely we will want to do the same thing Adam and Eve did. We will want to hide.

Simon Peter, Jesus' Disciple, who ultimately became the rock upon which the church was built, was not always a rock. Once when Peter was in the Presence of The Light of Jesus, he recognized the darkness within himself. As with Adam and Eve, Peter's first inclination was to get away from The Light.

When Simon Peter saw this,
he fell at Jesus' knees and said,
"Go away from me, Lord;
I am a sinful man!"
Luke 5:8 (NIV2011)

As Peter grew, he tried hard not to be a sinful man. In his growing pains, he resisted the thought that he needed to be bathed, especially by Jesus, who he hoped to impress. The day came when Jesus confronted Peter about his need to be bathed.

Then he [Jesus] poured water into a basin
and began to wash the disciples' feet
and dry them with the towel that he had tied around his waist.

When Jesus came to Simon Peter, Peter asked him,
"Lord, are you going to wash my feet?"

Jesus answered Peter,
"You don't know now what I'm doing.
You will understand later."

Peter told Jesus, "You will never wash my feet."

Jesus replied to Peter,
"If I don't wash you, you don't belong to me."

Simon Peter said to Jesus, "Lord, don't wash only my feet.
Wash my hands and my head too!"
John 13:5-9 (GW)

Would you trust The One to bathe you and prepare you for the ultimate intimate Life with Him? When He looks at you, He sees the fulfillment of all He created you to be. He sees His Glory reflected in you. For you were made in His Own Image.

So God created humans in his image.
In the image of God he created them.
He created them male and female.
Genesis 1:27 (GW)

He knows you and He loves you.

"…I have loved you with an everlasting love …"
Jeremiah 31:3 (NIV2011)
"…Never will I leave you;
never will I forsake you."
Hebrews 13:5 (NIV2011)
"…surely I am with you always …"
Matthew 28:20 (NIV2011)

Will you trust The One to be fully alive inside of you? Will you commit yourself to Him by saying back to Him the Words He is saying to you?

Chapter 22

How Will They Know You Love Me?

*A*fter we decide we want to commit to God and we get a tiny taste of His Glory, it seems natural that we want the world to see Him too. Like a newly engaged person, we want to show off the ring. We want people to know He chose us!

Sometimes we want to show off "God and me" instead of allowing God to introduce Himself in whatever way He chooses.

Moses, like Adam and Eve, had a close relationship with God. Moses became so close to God he felt he could speak frankly to God. Exodus, Chapter 33, Verses 12 through 21 detail an interesting conversation between Moses and God.

Moses was getting a bit anxious about leading the people God had given him to lead. Moses noted God had already told him He knew him by name and he had found favor with God. So He asked God for a little bit more.

> *"If you really are pleased with me, show me your ways*
> *so that I can know you and so that you will continue to be pleased with me.*
> *Remember: This nation is your people."*
> *Exodus 33:13 (GW)*

God promised to give Moses what he needed.

The LORD answered,
"My presence will go {with you,} and I will give you peace."
Exodus 33:14 (GW)

When God gives us His Very Self, His Presence, it will cover any need we ever have. However, Moses wanted further reassurance the people would see God's Presence with him.

Sometimes we seem to say to God, "OK, God, we know You and I are best friends, but it would help me get other people on track, if you could just sort of endorse me … You know, show up and put Your Arm around me … and do a few signs and wonders. And then I'm sure I could take it from there. They will have to believe what I say."

Often we want to be sure people are going to see God <u>with us</u>, instead of just wanting them to see God. If we are signing on to be the opening act for God, we want to be sure He comes on stage on time.

Then Moses said to him,
"If your presence is not going {with us},
don't make us leave this place.
How will anyone ever know you're pleased
with your people and me unless you go with us?
Then we will be different from all other people
on the face of the earth."
Exodus 33:15-16 (GW)

God again reassured Moses.

The LORD answered Moses,
"I will do what you have asked,
because I am pleased with you,

and I know you by name."
Exodus 33:17 (GW)

Moses got down to the crunch. He wanted visible evidence He could show other people to verify God.

Then Moses said, "Please let me see your glory."
Exodus 33:18 (GW)

Moses had started His Walk, just wanting to know God and to understand His Ways. But in his insecurity, He now wanted signs and wonders. Many times we begin by just wanting to know God and rest in His Love. We get glimpses of His Face. At times we actually may have goose bump types of experiences that tell us He is really with us.

And so we ask for more. Like Moses, we want to see all of God. And His Answers may frustrate us.

The LORD said,
"I will let all my goodness pass in front of you,
and there I will call out my name 'the LORD.'
I will be kind to anyone I want to.

I will be merciful to anyone I want to.
But you can't see my face,
because no one may see me and live."
Exodus 33:19-20 (GW)

God then hid Moses in the cleft of a rock and shielded him from looking directly at Him, as He passed by.

If God is our One and Only, why can't we see all of Him now? As with Moses, God has verified to us again and again that He will be present with us. It would be His Presence shining through Moses that the people would see. It will be

God inside of us that will put a smile on our face. It will be His Glory shining through us that the world will see!

Jesus told us how this relationship works.

> *"...I am in the Father and the Father is in me ..."*
> *John 14:11 (NIV2011)*

> *"...The words I say to you I do not speak on my own authority.*
> *Rather, it is the Father, living in me, who is doing his work."*
> *John 14:10 (NIV2011)*

> *"I have not spoken on my own.*
> *Instead, the Father who sent me told me what I should say*
> *and how I should say it.*
> *I know that what he commands is eternal life.*
> *Whatever I say is what the Father told me to say."*
> *John 12:49-50 (GW)*

Our relationship with God is personal and intimate. As we learn more and more about Him, He reveals more and more of Himself. When we discover the Joy of being in His Presence, we will find it to be more than enough. When we truly become one with Him, we will say what He says. We will live the Life He is living through us. We will no longer need to introduce Him. The world will see Him in us.

> *"...Anyone who has seen me has seen the Father ..."*
> *John 14:9 (NIV2011)*

Chapter 23

The Sizzling Current of True Love!

*G*od created male and female with the ability to function as One with Him and with each other in committed relationships. God created the human bodies of husband and wife to fit together physically, so "the two become one." Satan makes it his top priority to pervert what God has created as sacred.

Sometimes people are surprised to discover the Bible is full of rather explicit tales of sexual encounters, both the kind resulting from True Love and the kind satan had in mind when he whispered to Adam, "Quick! Hide your privates! God's coming!"

There are stories of incest, homosexuality, adultery mixed in with stories of True Love in committed marriages. If you want to settle in with a book of the Bible that has everything from action to comedy to raw sex, read the Song of Songs. There are some great lines in that book. My favorite is this description of a true dental wonder.

> *Your teeth are like a flock of sheep just shorn,*
> *coming up from the washing.*
> *Each has its twin;*
> *not one of them is alone.*
> *Song of Songs 4:2 (NIV2011)*

While some may feel God and sex should not even be mentioned in the same sentence, it was God Himself Who designed the male and female bodies to fit together in Holy Union with Him. If you have attempted to "make love" without ever thinking of The One Who truly did "make" (create) Love, then you may have missed the height of what He designed as a Celebration!

Even though translations of the Bible use the term, "making love," that phrase is really a misnomer. "Making love" implies we can create something only God can create. We cannot "make" love. Anything we would attempt to make on our own is only a cheap imitation of what God really had in mind.

When a husband and wife come together physically, it is a Celebration of Love. We can thank God for His amazing work in creating the perfect person for us, who brings us love and joy. We can thank God that He is present in every moment of our union and that He alone completes us.

The physical union of a man and woman, who are committed to God and to each other, is a symbolic picture of the spiritual Union they each have with God.

Initial "synching" begins with hugging, being close, heart to heart. When two people are close, their heartbeats tend to get into rate and rhythm with the other. Spiritually, when we get close to God, we get in synch with His Heart. We can relax and enjoy being close to Him.

Being face to face changes our focus from us to our partner. We can appreciate the facial expressions of the other. This is often followed by kissing. In kissing, our breathing pattern becomes similar, adding to the oneness. In a true Holy Celebration, The Breath of God flows between two of His Creations, who have committed themselves to Him and to each other.

In our spiritual relationship with God, we can experience the Joy of focusing on Him and feeling His Loving Focus on us. We can feel secure in His Love when we see Him up close and personal.

God designed the male anatomy to fit inside the female anatomy. God created in the man a connecting bridge to transport the male seeds of Life into the female to be connected with the seeds of Life waiting there. The Celebration of Love is intimate and private. Both parties are uncovered and open to the affections of the other. Both give and receive Love.

Sometimes God brings new life from the union of man and woman. God Our Creator designed the Seeds of Life to be housed within a male and a female. He furthered designed things in such a way that new life would not result except by the union of both the man and the woman with each other and with Him.

Spiritually, God also gave us a picture of The Love He brought to us through Jesus. We already had The Holy Spirit within us, but we may never have recognized Him. Jesus was the Bridge between what people thought they knew of God and Who He actually was. Jesus delivered the seeds of Life to us. New Life and Light were revealed!

God alone is the Author of Love, whether it be two people celebrating His Gift of Love to them, or whether God chooses to multiply that Love by creating a new Life through the woman becoming impregnated.

Satan has fought hard to reduce what God has created, to a lower level, where we attempt to keep God far away from our "sex life." So what happens in the Truest Celebration of Love? It happens, as the angel described to Mary. The Holy Spirit of God is right in the midst of the celebration!

> ..."*The Holy Spirit will come to you,*
> *and the power of the Most High will overshadow you. ...*"
> *Luke 1:35 (GW)*

God wants to overshadow everything else in our life. He wants to know us, in the true "Biblical sense." He is willing to give Himself to us and let us touch Him and know Him. He wants us to know He knows us completely, without any "fig leaves."

He wants to cover us with Himself and His Glory.

"On that day, you will realize that I am in my Father,
and you are in me,
and I am in you."
John 14:20 (NIV2011)

Chapter 24

Horrible Food Poisoning

*B*efore Adam and Eve could enjoy The Celebration of True Love, they needed more than a bath. They needed extensive healing. The effects of the evil to which they had been exposed had come to the surface. It was not a pretty sight.

The Bible is intriguing in the details it gives us. But it is also interesting that some details are deliberately not mentioned. As we read, we tend to splice in our own interpretations. Even translations of the Bible do not always agree. So, it is imperative that we ask The Holy Spirit to reveal to us what He wants us to understand.

I prefer the New International Version ©2011 (NIV) translation of what God did for Adam and Eve.

> *The LORD God made garments of skin*
> *for Adam and his wife*
> *and clothed them.*
> *Genesis 3:21 (NIV2011)*

Some believe God killed an animal and used the skin to cover Adam and Eve. They offer this as the first example of sacrifice to "save" someone.

However, I do not believe God wanted to set an example of killing, as a way to begin His World. He had not even killed satan. Why kill an innocent animal?

I do not believe God would use the skin of something foreign for His precious humans, who were made in His Own Image. He was and is The Creator! I believe, as the NIV Translation says, He <u>made</u> the garments of skin. He did not use scraps of something that already existed. He created a special covering for Adam and Eve. I believe that covering was a new human skin.

Did Adam and Eve have skin to begin with? If so, what had happened to their skin? I believe, after they ate the forbidden fruit, they may have developed a disease that was similar to leprosy.

Nowhere is it stated that Adam and Eve suffered from leprosy. However, it is interesting to consider whether it could have happened. The effects of the disease would have been just what satan ordered. The life of the leper was well described in Jesus' day.

Those who had leprosy were considered unclean and were forbidden to be around other people. They lived with other lepers in colonies. If they came in even remote contact with non-lepers, they were to yell out, "Unclean! Unclean!" Thus they not only were seen by others as unclean, but they were also forced to pronounce this judgment on themselves.

Leprosy is caused by bacteria that invade the body. It affects the nerves, respiratory tract, skin and eyes. This may result in an inability to feel pain. Parts of the body are sometimes lost, due to repeated injuries.[1]

Being able to feel and process information from the outside world is a blessing. Pain is the body's early warning sign that something is going on to which we need to give our attention. Satan does not want us to have any early warning signs of his invasions. Satan wants to be able to come in, undetected.

Satan would likely rejoice in the loss of any part of a human God had created. He would smile as they lost their sense of touch. He would laugh if they could no longer hold hands, hug or kiss.

Some might find God's pronouncement of pain as a part of the consequences for Adam and Eve to be a bit harsh. However, in pronouncing discipline on Adam and Eve that would involve pain and feeling, God was continuing to reverse the effects of what satan had done. He was restoring an early warning system.

Leprosy affects the respiratory system. As we have discussed, the Breath of God powers us. Satan would love to interfere with any life force of humans.

Satan loved the way God had originally created him to be beautiful. He had now fallen from his once beautiful heights to a pathetic creature, who crawled upon his belly. How it must have infuriated him that the humans he had had in the palm of his hands, now were with God, under His Protection. Satan despised their beauty. Leprosy was an illness that manifested itself in the skin. It was very disfiguring. People did not want to even look at those who had the illness.

Leprosy can also affect other parts of the body. In the early days of learning about leprosy, doctors often misdiagnosed it as syphilis. No wonder Adam and Eve wanted to cover up their private parts.

Leprosy can affect the mouth and tongue. Thus eating can become more difficult. Food that was once delicious becomes hard to eat.

And finally, leprosy can affect the eyes. Eyesight fails. Those affected are no longer able to enjoy those things they had found "pleasing to the eyes."[1]

Again, there is no verification that Adam and Eve suffered from a disease, such as leprosy, but it seems it would have been a slam-dunk for satan if they did. Simply covering themselves with fig leaves would not have healed Adam and Eve. Interestingly, fig leaves were used in many folk medicine remedies as a cure for skin diseases.

Adam and Eve needed more than leaf therapy. They needed the Touch of God within and without. They needed new undergarments and new outer garments.

1. "Leprosy." *Wikipedia: The Free Encyclopedia*. Wikimedia Foundation, Inc. 28 February 2015. Web. 9 March 2015. <https://en.wikipedia.org/wiki/Leprosy>

Chapter 25

Skin — A Covering Only God Could Create!

uman skin is an amazing organ. To detail some (not nearly all) of the functions of skin:

It acts as a barrier to toxic materials and foreign invaders. When an invader tries to enter the body, the skin screams.

It is a base for sensory reception. It can detect everything from a caress to a hard blow.

It is an immunologic source of hormones for protective cell differentiation.

It helps to regulate blood pressure and blood flow.

It actually absorbs substances and transfers them to other organs.

It regulates temperature.

It is involved in the metabolism and storage of fat.

It regulates water and salt metabolism through the process of sweating. (Adam was to learn more about sweating.)

It synthesizes important compounds, such as vitamin D.

It is an acidic barrier that protects against certain bacteria.

It is a self-cleanser.

The skin does all this and more.

God created skins of all types and colors. Just as He filled His World with different colors of plants and animals, so God also applied His Creative Palette of color to human skin. Satan hated the beauty of it all. He made it his priority to try to use skin color to create enmity and division between humans.

But God creates with unity. I believe God's covering for Adam and Eve was like the under covering of Jesus—seamless, without division. Look at the one visible part of your body that is seamless. It is your skin!

> *When the soldiers crucified Jesus,*
> *they took his clothes, dividing them into four shares,*
> *one for each of them,*
> *with the undergarment remaining.*
> *This garment was seamless,*
> *woven in one piece from top to bottom.*
> *John 19:23 (NIV2011)*

I believed God not only disciplined Adam and Eve, but He also forgave, healed and covered them. He carefully prepared them for the outside world they were about to experience.

Chapter 26

A Truth Satan Never Wanted You to Know

Satan knew about the human body. He knew all about God's Perfect Design for the body. It was satan's mission to assure humans never knew. He spent a great deal of his time thinking of ways these humans could defile their bodies.

Oh sure, God thought He had created such a unique way for these humans to express something called Love for each other. Satan had moments when God looked at him that he thought he remembered something God called Love. Sometimes when things were quiet, satan thought he could almost hear God saying to him, "I love you."

But satan quickly dismissed that thought. How could God love him? Even if it were possible, satan could not love God. Obviously God's brand of this thing He called Love involved obedience and surrender. Satan would never stoop to that level.

Satan knew a thousand ways already to get these humans to use their bodies in ways other than the one way God had designed. Satan laughed as he thought of it. Yeah, one day these humans would be paying him to get a little of the pleasure he could arrange for them through their bodies.

God taught Adam and Eve to beware of satan's schemes. Many years later, Paul would warn his followers.

Don't you realize that your bodies are parts of Christ's body?
Should I take the parts of Christ's body
and make them parts of a prostitute's body?
That's unthinkable!

Don't you realize that the person who unites himself with a prostitute
becomes one body with her?
God says, "The two will be one."
However, the person who unites himself with the Lord
becomes one spirit with him.
1 Corinthians 6:15-17 (GW)

When satan hears these words, he screams, "No! Unite with me! I'll give you more pleasure than you can ever imagine."

Stay away from sexual sins.
Other sins that people commit don't affect their bodies
the same way sexual sins do.
People who sin sexually sin against their own bodies.
Don't you know that your body is a temple
that belongs to the Holy Spirit?
The Holy Spirit, whom you received from God, lives in you.
You don't belong to yourselves.
1 Corinthians 6:18-19 (GW)

Satan would tempt the humans with pleasure for their bodies, but his goal was to enter their bodies and work from the inside. He wanted to turn The Temple into a Brothel.

Failing that, satan wanted to destroy The Temple from the outside. Every time it appeared he had won by torturing and killing a body, he gave his war cry, "Be afraid. Be very afraid! You will die!"

So the humans became very afraid of dying. Their lives, and ours today, became focused on staving off death. Humans came to see physical death as the worst thing that could happen to them.

> *Satan answered the LORD, "Skin for skin!*
> *Certainly, a man will give everything he has for his life."*
> *Job 2:4 (GW)*

But God had a Plan to deal with satan's every move. God would demonstrate over and over again that His Presence would be both inside The Temple and outside. In fact, God was to demonstrate that some boundaries were not what they appeared. The day would come when The Temple Doors would be blown open!

> *Since all of these sons and daughters have flesh and blood,*
> *Jesus took on flesh and blood to be like them.*
> *He did this so that by dying he would destroy*
> *the one who had power over death (that is, the devil).*
> *In this way he would free those who were slaves all their lives*
> *because they were afraid of dying.*
> *Hebrews 2:14-15 (GW)*

Jesus would show through His Own very public Death, that any power it appeared satan had was very limited. Satan could come against the outside of The Temple of The Holy Spirit, but once he tore through the outer wall, he would run right into the Power of The One! He would not only be stopped, but he would be totally defeated.

Chapter 27

Get Dressed! We're Going Outside!

$\mathcal{A}$dam and Eve had not heard all of God's Plan for their rehabilitation. Sadly, they would be leaving the Garden of Eden.

Then the LORD God said,
"The man has become like one of us,
since he knows good and evil.
He must not reach out and take the fruit from the tree of life and eat.
Then he would live forever."

So the LORD God sent the man out of the Garden of Eden
to farm the ground from which the man had been formed.
After he sent the man out,
God placed angels and a flaming sword that turned in all directions
east of the Garden of Eden.
He placed them there to guard the way to the tree of life.
Genesis 3:22-24 (GW)

Who was "us?" God, Jesus and The Holy Spirit—The Three in One.

Were Adam and Eve truly like God now? They were indeed made in the Image of God. However, they were only "like" God. They would never be God. And they were far from being mature. Allowing them access to the Tree of Life was an unacceptable risk.

God wanted His Children to have Eternal Life, not eternal death. He provided a way out of the temptation to eat from the Tree of Life.

> *There isn't any temptation that you have experienced*
> *which is unusual for humans.*
> *God, who faithfully keeps his promises,*
> *will not allow you to be tempted beyond your power to resist.*
> *But when you are tempted,*
> *he will also give you the ability to endure the temptation*
> *as your way of escape.*
> *1 Corinthians 10:13 (GW)*

God was sending Adam and Eve out into a world where satan and his demons were very active already. They would not be going alone. God would be with them every step of the way.

But before they stepped out of Eden's Gate, they needed to be dressed properly. God did provide new skin beneath their old diseased skin. It happened as our skin functions today. New skin grows beneath old, dying skin and pushes the old out of the way.

But God did more than provide an outer garment. He gave them undergarments, that were impervious to even the most vicious attack of satan. But they would have to keep their undergarments clean and in place. (Your mother was right—you need to wear clean underwear every day!)

Jesus' undergarment was seamless—unbroken. Even when Jesus' outer skin was pierced, those who pierced Him could not touch His Spirit! As long as we remain in God's Love, we will be eternally safe. Even if our outer covering is gone, the enemy will hit the wall of the seamless inner wall of The Spirit.

But if we become afraid because the enemy has breached the outer wall and we surrender or try to make a "deal with the devil," we will be open to satan's law of sin and death. If we choose to be with satan, then our eternal dwelling place will be with him as well. Jesus said plainly,

"Don't be afraid of those who kill the body
but cannot kill the soul.
Instead, fear the one who can destroy both body and soul in hell."
Matthew 10:28 (GW)

"My friends, I can guarantee that
you don't need to be afraid
of those who kill the body.
After that they can't do anything more.
I'll show you the one you should be afraid of.
Be afraid of the one who has the power
to throw you into hell after killing you.
I'm warning you to be afraid of him."
Luke 12:4-5 (GW)

Why does satan come again and again with attacks on the physical body? He entices humans to commit violence against each other, often deceiving them to do so in The Name of God. He entices people to commit violence against each other, even in families, in the name of discipline or control of a spouse.

Satan comes with various diseases, which attack the body. He brings torment and fear, as people battle against disabilities and death.

Satan deceives people into committing various lewd sexual acts, which tear at the very design of the beauty God created in the bodies of His Children.

Satan entices people to worship the bodies of others and to attempt to shape their own bodies into what they believe is beautiful. Satan entices them to strive for the approval of others instead of the approval of God.

Why does satan hate human bodies so much? Because he knows what he hopes humans never know.

Don't you know that your body is a temple that belongs to the Holy Spirit?
The Holy Spirit, whom you received from God, lives in you.
You don't belong to yourselves. You were bought for a price.
So bring glory to God in the way you use your body.
1 Corinthians 6:19-20 (GW)

Our Bodies are a Temple! Our Bodies are the Home of The Holy Spirit, Who God breathed into our bodies from our beginning. Satan knows there is a spiritual undergarment behind the skin. He knows as long as we keep the shields up, he will never successfully enter in. However, if he can scare us into giving up and opening the door to him, he is home free.

He comes again and again to attack and shake the outsides of what is God's Temple.

How can we resist satan?

Chapter 28

Temple Under Attack!

*W*e need not fear death of the earthly body. The earthly body is a wonderful "mobile home," created by God for a season. Like all parts of the body, it functions as long as God decrees.

David the Psalmist said,

> *… Every day {of my life} was recorded in your book*
> *before one of them had taken place.*
> *Psalm 139:16 (GW)*

I interpret David's statement to mean that God has predetermined how many days we will live on earth. We are like space travelers, who are sent on a mission with just enough oxygen to last for the mission.

Will God ever change His Mind about how long we will live on earth? Yes, He could. There is some biblical evidence that seems to indicate God changed His Plans at times. However, the key point is that God alone sets the limits of our living and our dying. We do not. Satan does not.

However, we can affect the quality of life we will have within those boundaries. We can affect the choices we make during the time we are here on earth. Satan cannot make us do anything. But he can entice us to let him in. Once we give him permission to enter, we will find he speaks loudly. We will find we agree with him more and more often. And life will be a downhill spiral into destruction.

If we keep our guard up and stay true to God, will this life be trouble free? Will life on easy street be our reward for making a good choice? No. Satan will continue to attack. He will continue to deceive and affect the way we look at our circumstances. Satan will continue to use every tactic he has to lure us away from God and to himself.

When he comes at us again and again, he will be hoping we will believe God has forsaken us. He will be hoping we will then give up and he can subdue us.

Jesus did not mince Words about the state of a world with satan and his demons running around in it.

"In the world you'll have trouble.
But cheer up! I have overcome the world."
John 16:33 (GW)

Satan will continue to shake the outside of The Temple, but he cannot get through the internal Spiritual Wall, as long as we wear our God Given Spiritual Underwear!

Chapter 29

The Precious Undergarment

*P*aul gave us specific instructions for how to keep our Spiritual Wall intact.

Finally, be strong in the Lord and in his mighty power.
Put on the full armor of God,
so that you can take your stand against the devil's schemes.
For our struggle is not against flesh and blood,
but against the rulers,
against the authorities,
against the powers of this dark world
and against the spiritual forces of evil in the heavenly realms.

Therefore put on the full armor of God,
so that when the day of evil comes,
you may be able to stand your ground,
and after you have done everything, to stand.
Stand firm then,
with the belt of truth buckled around your waist,
with the breastplate of righteousness in place,
and with your feet fitted with the readiness
that comes from the gospel of peace.

In addition to all this,
take up the shield of faith,
with which you can extinguish all the flaming arrows of the evil one.
Take the helmet of salvation and
The sword of the Spirit, which is the word of God.

And pray in the Spirit on all occasions
with all kinds of prayers and requests.
With this in mind,
be alert
and always keep on praying for all the Lord's people.
Ephesians 6:10-18 (NIV2011)

Paul effectively laid out the battle plan. Now let's look at some key points.

WHEN the day of evil comes …

Paul tells us "when the day of evil comes." Jesus told us there would be trouble in this world. Don't go off and breathe in satan's wacky weed, paint a few 60's type peace signs and zone out on the good times. If you don't feel satan's presence right now, be thankful, but the day of evil will manifest itself. Be on guard!

Not by our might, but by THE POWER OF GOD!

You cannot hold up the Spiritual Wall in your own strength. Your only strength is God's Strength. Your only power is God's Power. Your part is surrendering to your Commanding Officer and following His Orders immediately and completely.

The FULL Armor of God

You must put on The FULL Armor of God. If you miss even one part of your uniform, you will be a sitting duck for satan. FULL Armor means keeping all the parts of The Armor of God in place.

The Belt of Truth

Adam and Eve had the urge to protect their private parts. God is interested in protecting our private parts too. They are the sites of His Instruments of Creation. The function of a belt is to hold one's pants up. In order to fulfill its function, a belt must be firmly buckled in place.

Jesus frequently punctuated what He said with the preface, "I tell you The Truth." He wanted us to understand that our life was dependent on knowing the Real Truth. He was Truth. Satan was not.

Jesus answered,
"I am the way and the truth and the life ..."
John 14:6 (NIV2011)

[Jesus, speaking of satan]
"... He was a murderer from the beginning,
not holding to the truth, for there is no truth in him.
When he lies, he speaks his native language,
for he is a liar and the father of lies."
John 8:44 (NIV2011)

The Breastplate of Righteousness

The Breastplate not only protects the breasts, but it protects the heart and lungs. It protects the ribs. The breasts of the female, figuratively speaking, are the source of nourishment for the baby. The source of our spiritual nourishment must be protected.

The heart and lungs are part of the center of life. If the heart or lungs are irreparably damaged, the body ceases to function. It is the same in the Spiritual Body. If your heart for the Lord and His People are damaged or you stop breathing the Breath of The Holy Spirit, which is in you, Life in the Spirit will stop.

Without the full protection of our Spiritual Armor, we would be forced to try to stand in our own righteousness. Here's the bad news about that.

> *Indeed, there is no one on earth who is righteous,*
> *no one who does what is right and never sins.*
> *Ecclesiastes 7:20 (NIV2011)*

When God told Abraham he was going to have a son, Abraham believed all God told him, even though to his natural mind it would have seemed like foolishness. Abraham and Sarah were thought to be too old to have a child and yet God told them it was so.

Even though Abraham had no righteousness in himself, God was pleased that Abraham simply believed God. The Bible says, God "credited" Abraham's faith as "righteousness." The good news is God is willing to do the same for us, if we will simply believe Him, and His Words sent through Jesus, and brought to our remembrance by The Holy Spirit.

> *This is why "it was credited to him as righteousness."*
> *The words "it was credited to him"*
> *were written not for him alone, but also for us,*
> *to whom God will credit righteousness—*
> *for us who believe in him who raised Jesus our Lord from the dead.*
> *He was delivered over to death for our sins*
> *and was raised to life for our justification.*
> *Romans 4:22-25 (NIV2011)*

God protects our hearts with His Righteousness. We need to keep our Spiritual Breastplate in place. We need to continue to believe God, even when circumstances seem contrary to what He said.

> *Above all else, guard your heart,*
> *for everything you do flows from it.*
> *Proverbs 4:23 (NIV2011)*

Feet Fitted with the Readiness that Comes from the Gospel of Peace

How do good soldiers know what to do when they are surprised by the enemy? They have trained ahead of time. They have their weapons loaded and they know how to use them. They don't wait until there is a crisis and then yell for someone to go find the manual that might say what to do in such a situation.

Unfortunately many of us treat God like a 9-1-1 Emergency Operator. When we get in a pinch, we get on the horn and scream "Help!" Or we grab a Bible and try opening it multiple times at random to try to piece together a message from God.

God wants us to be ready for the day of evil. He does not want us to be wishy-washy and try to fend off the devil ourselves. He wants us to understand that the best weapon in our arsenal is His Word. But we have to pack it inside of us ahead of time. And we have to listen closely to The Holy Spirit to know which Words to use and at what exact moment and circumstance.

The Message Jesus brought us, as recorded in the Gospels, was and is a Message of Peace. God wants us to take every Word and store it deep inside the Temple. He wants us to review it often and let it soak into our inner thoughts so deeply that no attack of satan can dislodge it. When The Holy Spirit brings to mind which Words to use, we need to be ready to move!

Shield of Faith

What is faith? Paul, as recorded in Hebrews, Chapter 11, describes faith.

> *Now faith is confidence in what we hope for*
> *and assurance about what we do not see.*
> *Hebrews 11:1 (NIV2011)*

We often hear the declaration; "I'll believe it when I see it."

However, a much deeper Truth of The Spirit is "I'll see it when I believe it!"

When we are willing to believe God, simply because He says so, we will have the beginnings of faith. It is both amazing and amusing to see how many things God delighted to do by making them seem impossible by human standards.

Yet when God's People were willing to simply do what God said to do, because He said to do it, they saw amazing results. Faith comes down to whether we trust God.

Paul taught about the Armor of God long after Adam and Eve. But, God's Words never change. The Words He gave to Paul likely were Words He had already shared with Adam and Eve and now shares with us today.

Chapter 30

Traveling Orders

*A*s God sent Adam and Eve out of the Garden of Eden, His Message was for them, as it is for us. Trust and Obey!

Jeremiah, the Prophet, and Solomon, the author of Proverbs, wrote after the time of Adam and Eve. However, once again, remember God's Words are timeless. His Words reach backwards and forwards in time.

I imagine God gave Adam and Eve a pep talk before leading them out of the garden. He is here now with these Words for you.

> *I know the plans that I have for you, declares the LORD.*
> *They are plans for peace and not disaster,*
> *plans to give you a future filled with hope.*
> *Jeremiah 29:11 (GW)*

> *My son, do not forget my teaching,*
> *but keep my commands in your heart,*
> *for they will prolong your life many years*
> *and bring you peace and prosperity.*

Let love and faithfulness never leave you;
bind them around your neck,
write them on the tablet of your heart.
Then you will win favor and a good name
in the sight of God and man.

Trust in the LORD with all your heart
and lean not on your own understanding;
in all ways submit to him,
and he will make your paths straight.

Do not be wise in your own eyes;
fear the LORD and shun evil.
This will bring health to your body
and nourishment to your bones.

Honor the LORD with your wealth,
with the first fruits of all your crops;
then your barns will be filled to overflowing,
and your vats will brim over with new wine.

My son, do not despise the LORD's discipline,
and do not resent his rebuke,
because the LORD disciplines those he loves,
as a father the son he delights in.

Blessed are those who find wisdom,
those who gain understanding,
for she is more profitable than silver
and yields better returns than gold.
She is more precious than rubies;
nothing you desire can compare with her.
Long life is in her right hand;
in her left hand are riches and honor.

Her ways are pleasant ways,
and all her paths are peace.
She is a tree of life to those who take hold of her;
those who hold her fast will be blessed.

By wisdom the Lord laid the earth's foundations,
by understanding he set the heavens in place;
by his knowledge the watery depths were divided,
and the clouds let drop the dew.
My son, do not let wisdom and understanding out of your sight,
preserve sound judgment and discretion;
they will be life for you,
an ornament to grace your neck.
Then you will go on your way in safety,
and your foot will not stumble.
When you lie down, you will not be afraid;
when you lie down, your sleep will be sweet.
Have no fear of sudden disaster
or of the ruin that overtakes the wicked,
for the LORD will be at your side
and will keep your foot from being snared.
Proverbs 3:1-26 (NIV2011)

Jesus, in His Prayer to His Father, shortly before His Crucifixion, told God He was not asking that we be removed from the world. Indeed, we are here as His Missionaries.

[Jesus speaking to His Father]
"I'm not asking you to take them out of the world
but to protect them from the evil one.
They don't belong to the world any more
than I belong to the world.

115

"Use the truth to make them holy.
Your words are truth.
I have sent them into the world the same way you sent me into the world."
John 17:15-18 (GW)

God wants us to be able to say, as did Jesus,

"On earth I have given you glory
by finishing the work you gave me to do.
Now, Father, give me glory in your presence
with the glory I had with you before the world existed."
John 17:4-5 (GW)

God has a Plan for our lives. It is a good Plan. We can trust Him. We are in a world where Good and Evil are both present. We were not exiled here. We are never alone. God is with us at every moment. We have been sent here to turn on the Lights and eliminate the darkness, one light at a time. Are you ready?

When Jesus spoke again to the people,
he said,
"I am the light of the world.
Whoever follows me will never walk in darkness,
but will have the light of life."
John 8:12 (NIV2011)

"You are the light of the world.
A town built on a hill cannot be hidden.
Neither do people light a lamp and put it under a bowl.
Instead they put it on its stand,
and it gives light to everyone in the house.
In the same way, let your light shine before others,
that they may see your good deeds
and glorify your Father in heaven."
Matthew 5:14-16 (NIV2011)

Who is God?

" …God is love."
1 John 4:8 (NIV2011)

" …And he will be called
Wonderful Counselor,
Mighty God,
Everlasting Father,
Prince of Peace."
Isaiah 9:6 (NIV2011)

For there are three
that bear record in heaven,
the Father, the Word, and the Holy Ghost:
and these three are one.
1 John 5:7 (KJV)

Chapter 1

Can Humans See God?

Most of us have heard about God since we were small. But how we saw God probably changed as we grew. Does God change? No.

> *"I, the LORD, never change. ..."*
> *Malachi 3:6 (GW)*

But how God reveals Himself may change. He comes to us in different ways at different times, always with an approach that is just right for that time in our lives. If it is gentle encouragement we need, He will provide. If it is a huge stop sign right in front of us, He will provide that too.

> *"I am going to do something new.*
> *It is already happening. Don't you recognize it? ..."*
> *Isaiah 43:19 (GW)*

God can never be put in a box. If you start believing you have found someone with all the answers about God, beware. Jesus warned that there would be plenty of people, who would try to limit God to one time or one place. Impossible!

Jesus said to his disciples,
"The time will come when you will long to see
one of the days of the Son of Man, but you will not see it.
People will say, 'There he is!' or 'Here he is!'
Don't run after those people.
The day of the Son of Man will be like lightning
that flashes from one end of the sky to the other."
Luke 17:22-24 (GW)

Let's look at some of the ways God appeared on earth. Being the Ultimate Creator, He showed up in places people never expected to find Him. And He showed His Presence by doing things no one else had ever done.

He showed His Presence in personal ways. He guided and guarded. He rescued. And at times, He stopped people, saving them from destruction.

God made Himself very visible in the heavens and on the earth.

<u>God revealed Himself to Jacob through a dream.</u>

Jacob was on his way from Beersheba to Harran. He stopped for the night.

...He took one of the stones from that place,
put it under his head, and lay down there.
He had a dream in which he saw a stairway set up on the earth
with its top reaching up to heaven.
He saw the angels of God going up and coming down on it.
The LORD was standing above it, saying,
"I am the LORD, the God of your
grandfather Abraham and the God of Isaac. ..."
Genesis 28:11-13 (GW)

<u>God revealed Himself to Moses through a burning bush.</u>

The Messenger of the LORD appeared to him there
as flames of fire coming out of a bush.
Moses looked, and although the bush was on fire,
it was not burning up.
So he thought, "Why isn't this bush burning up?
I must go over there and see this strange sight."
When the LORD saw that Moses had come over to see it,
God called to him from the bush, "Moses, Moses!" …
Exodus 3:2-4 (GW)

<u>God revealed Himself to the Children of Israel through</u>
<u>a Pillar of Cloud and a Pillar of Fire.</u>

By day the LORD went ahead of them
in a pillar of cloud to guide them on their way
and by night in a pillar of fire to give them light,
so that they could travel by day or night.
Exodus 13:21 (NIV2011)

<u>God revealed Himself to Jonah in the belly of a whale.</u>

The LORD sent a big fish to swallow Jonah.
Jonah was inside the fish for three days and three nights.
Jonah 1:17 (GW)

<u>God revealed Himself to Elijah through a gentle whisper.</u>

God said, "Go out and stand in front of the LORD on the mountain."
As the LORD was passing by, a fierce wind tore mountains
and shattered rocks ahead of the LORD.
But the LORD was not in the wind.
After the wind came an earthquake.

121

But the LORD wasn't in the earthquake.
After the earthquake there was a fire.
But the LORD wasn't in the fire.
And after the fire there was a quiet, whispering voice.
1 Kings 19:11-12 (GW)

<u>God revealed Himself to Samuel by calling him directly by name.</u>

Samuel had no experience with the LORD,
because the word of the LORD had not yet been revealed to him.

The LORD called Samuel a third time.
Samuel got up, went to Eli, and said,
"Here I am. You called me."
Then Eli realized that the LORD was calling the boy.
"Go, lie down," Eli told Samuel.
"When he calls you, say, 'Speak, LORD. I'm listening.'"
So Samuel went and lay down in his room.

The LORD came and stood there.
He called as he had called the other times: "Samuel! Samuel!"
And Samuel replied, "Speak. I'm listening."
1 Samuel 3:8-10 (GW)

<u>God revealed Himself to Job by allowing him to have trials</u>

Job was a righteous man, or so he thought. God allowed satan to test him. Initially Job did well, but under continued pressure, he cracked like an egg. He was finally into the ultimate argument with God. God allowed Job to go on and on before God spoke.

Chapters 38 through 42 of the book of Job detail what God said. After hearing all God had to say, Job knew, beyond a shadow of a doubt that he had been in the Presence of Almighty God.

Then Job answered the LORD,
"I know that you can do everything
and that your plans are unstoppable.
"{You said,} 'Who is this that belittles my advice
without having any knowledge {about it}?'
Yes, I have stated things I didn't understand,
things too mysterious for me to know.
"{You said,} 'Listen now, and I will speak.
I will ask you, and you will teach me.'
I had heard about you with my own ears,
but now I have seen you with my own eyes.
That is why I take back what I said,
and I sit in dust and ashes to show that I am sorry."
Job 42:1-6 (GW)

<u>God revealed Himself to the Pharaoh</u>
<u>by having Moses repeatedly bring God's Word of Warning.</u>
<u>God then revealed Himself by bringing plagues.</u>

It is not in God's Nature to mess with people and make them miserable for His Enjoyment. However, God does allow unpleasant things to happen at times, in order to accomplish His Perfect Will.

At the direction of God, Moses repeatedly went to the Pharaoh, delivering The Word of God and imploring him to let God's People go. The Pharaoh repeatedly refused.

God brought upon the Pharaoh and his household a total of ten plagues. You can read all about it in Exodus, Chapters 7 through 11.

God revealed Himself to Moses
by personally writing The Ten Commandments.

The LORD finished speaking to Moses on Mount Sinai.
Then he gave him the two tablets with his words on them,
stone tablets inscribed by God himself.
Exodus 31:18 (GW)

God revealed Himself to Ezekiel
by giving him vivid and detailed visions.

You can read the more complete version in Ezekiel, Chapter 1. His vision concluded with his recognition of God.

A voice came from above the dome over their heads
as they stood still with their wings lowered.
Above the dome over their heads was something
that looked like a throne made of sapphire.
On the throne was a figure that looked like a human.
Then I saw what he looked like from the waist up.
He looked like glowing bronze with fire all around it.
From the waist down, he looked like fire.
A bright light surrounded him.
The brightness all around him looked like a rainbow in the clouds.
It was like the LORD'S glory.
When I saw it, I immediately bowed down,
and I heard someone speaking.
Ezekiel 1:25-28 (GW)

God revealed Himself to David the Psalmist in multiple ways.
One of those ways was to allow David to see Him inside of David.

As recorded in Psalm, Chapter 139, David discovered that God had been with him since his creation. He marveled at how God was still constantly with him, knowing everything about him.

Please read all of Psalm, Chapter 139 to see how much God revealed to David, who said,

I will give thanks to you because
I have been so amazingly and miraculously made.
Your works are miraculous,
and my soul is fully aware of this.
Psalm 139:14 (GW)

<u>God revealed to David</u>
<u>how He reveals Himself throughout His Creation.</u>
The heavens declare the glory of God,
and the sky displays what his hands have made.
One day tells a story to the next.
One night shares knowledge with the next
without talking, without words,
without their voices being heard.

{Yet,} their sound has gone out into the entire world,
their message to the ends of the earth. ...
Psalm 19:1-4 (GW)

<u>God revealed to Paul</u>
<u>how He reveals Himself throughout His Creation.</u>

What can be known about God is clear to them
because he has made it clear to them.
From the creation of the world, God's invisible qualities,
his eternal power and divine nature,
have been clearly observed in what he made.
As a result, people have no excuse.
Romans 1:19-20 (GW)

We can see in these examples how God revealed Himself in different ways. There are many more examples all throughout the Bible of God's Creative Ways of revealing Himself.

Often the people of earth did not recognize God. It took more than human sight to see Him. God's Ways are higher than our ways and His Thoughts higher than our thoughts. When His Children were ready and willing, God was ready and willing to raise them to that higher place where they could see Him with their spiritual eyes. He will do the same for us.

In the fullness of time, God took Creation up many notches, as He created a human Body for Himself. God had been on earth all along. God had been visible. God had spoken. But there came a glorious time when He chose to be visible through human eyes and heard through human ears. He chose to touch and be touched through human hands. Humans saw the Life He had for them, as He lived it in front of them as a human. God revealed Himself on earth as a man known as Jesus!

However, before we consider how and why God came as Jesus, let's look at the unique way God Himself is made. God is One and yet Three. How can this be?

Chapter 2

How Can Three Be One?

$\mathcal{M}$any of us have been taught God, Jesus and The Holy Spirit together form The Trinity. As we read the Bible, we can see all Three in evidence. However, as we try to grasp how the Three in One work, often the best we can do is imagine them as a team of three. Some believe the members of that team can never be on earth's stage at the same time.

The following is the scenario some use to explain The Actions of The Trinity. (*Note: I do not agree with this scenario!*)

God came first. He was primarily in Heaven, but came to earth now and then. God then retired to Heaven and sent Jesus to earth. Jesus was in close contact with God, but not necessarily One with Him. Jesus appeared to have been killed, but came back to life. He then left earth to be with God in Heaven. Some time passed and the people on earth were sort of on their own. They tried to help each other out to get through life. Then The Holy Spirit came. Jesus will come back to earth on some future unknown day.

As we try to keep up with Who is where and when, we often end up confused.

Before we look closer at how The One actually functions as One, let's consider ourselves. Are you three in one? It's quite possible you are even more than three persons in one body! How can this be?

You might be a child of your parents, a parent to your children, a grandparent of your grandchildren, someone's spouse, and on and on. You are all those people in one body. The fact that you are a parent to a child does not mean that you leave your body as a child of a parent. No, you are one! You serve in different roles at different times. You do all of this from one body.

The parts of our physical body cannot be separated in their natural created state. Unless you have surgery or some other invasive event, your liver will remain in the same body as your lungs and other parts. Each part will perform its function, but together they will be inseparable in one body.

First Corinthians, Chapter 12 records Paul's words to explain how The Body of Christ has many parts, but is one Body.

> *For example, the body is one unit and yet has many parts.*
> *As all the parts form one body, so it is with Christ.*
> *By one Spirit we were all baptized into one body. ...*
> *1 Corinthians 12:12-13 (GW)*

We can recognize the different functions of The Father, The Son and The Holy Spirit, but, as with The Body, they are inseparable. They have always been together. They are together right now. They shall be together eternally.

Chapter 3

But I Thought The Bible Said ...

"Wait!" you might say. "Aren't there specific scriptures that verify God, Jesus and The Holy Spirit were in different places at different times?" On a first look, it might appear that way. Let's look closer.

For God did not send his Son into the world to condemn the world,
but to save the world through him.
John 3:17 (NIV2011)

<u>If God *sent* Jesus into the world, wouldn't that mean They were separate?</u> Not necessarily. In order to move our physical leg, the brain must send a command through the nerves to the muscles, which pull on the bones to move our leg. All those parts are functioning together in one body and all are working toward the same goal.

<u>When Jesus was talking to God, was He talking to Himself?</u> No, He was speaking as One with God and The Holy Spirit. God, Jesus and The Holy Spirit speak as One.

Here is an example. Let's consider a person named John Edward Smith. He might be known to his family as John Smith. But after he grew up, he decided to go by Edward Smith. When John's family and John's new friends are together and John Edward Smith speaks, who is speaking?

Both John and Edward are speaking. Are either John or Edward talking to themselves? No! They are speaking as one. And the one person is speaking for the benefit of those listening to him speak.

Not only did Jesus say over and over again that He was One with The Father, but God imbedded His Name into Jesus' full name. Besides being named Jesus, Jesus was also named Immanuel. The Name, *Immanuel*, identified Who He was. The Name, *Jesus*, identified His Mission.

> *"The virgin will conceive and give birth to a son,*
> *and they will call him Immanuel"*
> *(which means "God with us").*
> *Matthew 1:23 (NIV2011)*

> *"She will give birth to a son,*
> *and you are to give him the name Jesus,*
> *because he will save his people from their sins."*
> *Matthew 1:21 (NIV2011)*

The One was speaking, so those hearing would know how they also could communicate with God.

> *... He left you an example*
> *so that you could follow in his footsteps.*
> *1 Peter 2:21 (GW)*

> *So faith comes from hearing the message,*
> *and the message that is heard is what Christ spoke.*
> *Romans 10:17 (GW)*

Then Jesus said,
"Whoever has ears to hear,
let them hear."
Mark 4:9 (NIV2011)

Jesus showed us how to relate to God, so we could experience the Joy of being connected in True Love.

"… but I say these things while I am still in the world,
so that they may have the full measure of my joy within them."
John 17:13 (NIV2011)

"I have made you known to them,
and will continue to make you known
in order that the love you have for me may be in them
and I myself may be in them."
John 17:26 (NIV2011)

<u>Didn't Jesus say He had to leave before The Holy Spirit would come?</u>

"However, I am telling you the truth:
It's good for you that I'm going away.
If I don't go away, the helper won't come to you.
But if I go, I will send him to you."
John 16:7 (GW)

Consider this example. Imagine a pot with water in it. We take some of the water out of the pot, freeze it into ice cubes and put it back in the water. The water and the ice were and are one. They are together, but in different forms.

Now, let's heat the water to boiling. We cannot do that without melting the ice. The ice melts into the water. It is still one, but has changed form.

As the water heats up more and more, steam is formed from the water. It is still one, but is now in yet another form. For the steam to appear, the ice had to melt. The water was one from the beginning to the end. But it changed forms. And, so it is with God, Jesus, and The Holy Spirit. They are together, but able to change forms to accomplish their goals in the best way.

God came to earth as Jesus to fulfill His Mission of saving people from their sins. However, it was never His Plan to limit Himself to just one human body in one specific time and place. After God had accomplished His Mission through Jesus, it was time for Him to reveal Himself through the lives of others, who now knew He lived inside of them.

Did Jesus go away? No, His Outer Covering went away. But He was still very present in The One. The One simply changed form to begin the next part of The Mission to change the world.

So why would it even matter that we understand God, Jesus and The Holy Spirit are One? It matters because that One Truth will affect all of how you view God, Jesus and The Holy Spirit. And it may turn upside down many of the things you always thought you knew about Them.

> *...The LORD our God,*
> *The LORD is one.*
> *Deuteronomy 6:4 (NIV2011)*

> *Then Jesus declared,*
> *"I, the one*
> *speaking to you—*
> *I am he."*
> *John 4:26 (NIV2011)*

Chapter 4

Together From The Beginning, Now and Forever!

*L*et's go back to the beginning of Time, as we understand Time from The Bible. Let's look at how God, Jesus and The Holy Spirit were One. I will add emphasis to each part of the Scripture that demonstrates the Three working as One.

> *In the beginning <u>God</u> created heaven and earth.*
> *The earth was formless and empty,*
> *and darkness covered the deep water.*
> *<u>The Spirit of God</u> was hovering over the water.*
> *Genesis 1:1-2 (GW)*

How did God bring about the awesome work of Creation? He spoke! God spoke and His Words brought forth Life!

> *In the beginning was <u>the Word</u>,*
> *and*
> *<u>the Word</u> was with <u>God</u>,*
> *and*
> *<u>the Word was God.</u>*
>
> *<u>He was with God in the beginning.</u>*
> *Through him all things were made;*

without him nothing was made that has been made.

In him was <u>life</u>,
and that life was <u>the light</u> of all mankind.
John 1:1-4 (NIV2011)

Who was identified as The Light of the World? <u>Jesus</u>!

" ...<u>I am the light of the world.</u>
Whoever follows me will never walk in darkness,
but will have <u>the light of life</u>."
John 8:12 (NIV2011)

To further clarify Who Jesus, The Word, was —

<u>The Word</u> became flesh and made his dwelling among us.
We have seen his glory,
the glory of the one and only <u>Son</u>,
who came from <u>the Father</u>,
full of grace and truth.
John 1:14 (NIV2011)

God assured we would know Who He was. As we have seen, He appeared in different ways to different people before Jesus was visible on the earth. But God also made sure we would know Him in the Person of Jesus!

For to us a child is born,
to us a <u>son</u> is given,
and the government will be on his shoulders.
And <u>he will be called</u>
<u>Wonderful Counselor,</u>
<u>Mighty God, Everlasting Father,</u>
<u>Prince of Peace.</u>
Isaiah 9:6 (NIV2011)

"The virgin will conceive and give birth to a <u>son</u>,
and they will call him Immanuel"
(which means "<u>God with us</u>").
Matthew 1:23-24 (NIV2011)

Jesus testified to His Oneness with the Father.

"<u>I and the Father are one.</u>"
John 10:30 (NIV2011)

Jesus answered, "I am the way and the truth and the life.
<u>No one comes to the Father except through me.</u>
<u>If you really know me, you will know my Father as well.</u>
<u>From now on, you do know him and have seen him.</u>"

Philip said, "Lord, show us the Father and that will be enough for us."

Jesus answered:
"Don't you know me, Philip,
even after I have been among you such a long time?
<u>Anyone who has seen me has seen the Father.</u>
How can you say, 'Show us the Father'?
Don't you believe that <u>I am in the Father,</u>
<u>and that the Father is in me</u>?
The words I say to you I do not speak on my own authority.
Rather, it is <u>the Father, living in me, who is doing his work.</u>"
John 14:6-10 (NIV2011)

"On that day you will realize that <u>I am in my Father,</u>
and you are in me,
and I am in you."
John 14:20 (NIV2011)

Paul testified of The One.

> *There is <u>one body and one Spirit</u>,*
> *just as you were called to one hope when you were called;*
> <u>*one Lord*</u>*, one faith, one baptism;*
> <u>*one God and Father*</u> *of all,*
> *who is over all and through all and in all.*
> *Ephesians 4:4-6 (NIV2011)*

God The Creator, The Spirit of God, and The Word that "was God" were together from the beginning. They are now and ever more shall be!

Most miraculously, They are in us too! We'll talk about the wonder of how The Three in One are really The Many in One in future chapters. But now, let's look at The Shared Name of The One.

Chapter 5

Sharing A Unique Name

N ames have been very important to God from the beginning. He named Adam and Eve. He allowed Adam to name all the animals. There is even evidence that God named each of the stars and called them by name.

> *He determines the number of stars.*
> *He gives each one a name.*
> Psalm 147:4 (GW)

God named you!

> ... *"Do not fear, for I have redeemed you;*
> *I have called you by name; you are Mine!"*
> Isaiah 43:1 (NASB)

God named Himself! Through His Name He sent The Message that He is timeless and ever present.

> *Then Moses replied to God, "Suppose I go to the people of Israel and*
> *say to them,*
> *'The God of your ancestors has sent me to you,'*

and they ask me, 'What is his name?'
What should I tell them?"

God answered Moses, "I Am Who I Am.
This is what you must say to the people of Israel:
'I Am has sent me to you.'"

Again God said to Moses,
"This is what you must say to the people of Israel:
The LORD God of your ancestors,
the God of Abraham, Isaac, and Jacob, has sent me to you.
This is my name forever.
This is my title throughout every generation."
Exodus 3:13-15 (GW)

What can we learn about God from His Name? He is timeless and ever present. The declarative phrase "I AM" will always be part of a sentence that is in the present. God's Name is not "I was," "I used to be," or even "I will be." Whatever He was, He is right now and shall ever be.

What God was in Moses' time, He is in our present time, and will be in each moment of our future.

In giving us His Name, God has indeed given us access to Him and His Mighty Power. When a woman marries a man, often she places his name at the end of her name to indicate her new relationship. Example: Mary Smith marries John Jones. Mary adds his name and now is known as Mary Smith Jones.

In our relationship with God, we always put His Name before ours. Therefore, when we say "I AM" with anything following, we are using God's Name to verify what we say. This Blessed Union is His Going Before us to make our words true, if our words line up with Who He is.

Example:
I AM loving. I AM faithful. I AM healed. I AM at peace.

God always agrees with us when we speak His Truth! Jesus only spoke God's Truth. He completely agreed with all God said and God therefore, agreed with all Jesus said.

Jesus responded to them,
"What I teach doesn't come from me but from the one who sent me."
John 7:16 (GW)

So Jesus told them,
"When you have lifted up the Son of Man,
then you'll know that I am the one
and that I can't do anything on my own.
Instead, I speak as the Father taught me."
John 8:28 (GW)

"I have not spoken on my own.
Instead, the Father who sent me told me
what I should say and how I should say it.
I know that what he commands is eternal life.
Whatever I say is what the Father told me to say."
John 12:49-50 (GW)

"Don't you believe that I am in the Father,
and that the Father is in me?
The words I say to you I do not speak on my own authority.
Rather, it is the Father, living in me, who is doing his work."
John 14:10 (NIV2011)

The Holy Spirit, likewise, agrees with God and Jesus, and they agree with Him.

"When the Advocate comes, whom I will send to you from the Father—
the Spirit of truth who goes out from the Father—
he will testify about me."
John 15:26 (NIV2011)

When we agree with God, Jesus and The Holy Spirit, we can be confident it will be done, as we have asked in faith.

We are confident that God listens to us
if we ask for anything that has his approval.
We know that he listens to our requests.
So we know that we already have what we ask him for.
1 John 5:14-15 (GW)

However, if we place what is not true of God after His Name of "I AM," not only will it be a lie, but it will bring evil back to us. Remember how Jesus identified satan.

"...He was a murderer from the beginning, not holding to the truth,
for there is no truth in him.
When he lies, he speaks his native language,
for he is a liar and the father of lies."
John 8:44 (NIV2011)

When we use God's Name of "I AM" and we speak that which is not true of God, we are misusing God's Name. God will not agree with us. However satan will agree. Satan will jump up and down and yell, "I agree!" Evil is headed your way.

Examples:
"I am mad." "I am depressed." "I am defeated." God is none of these.

In the giving of the Ten Commandments, God was very clear He expected His Name to be used correctly.

*"You shall not misuse the name of the LORD your God,
for the LORD will not hold anyone guiltless who misuses his name."
Exodus 20:7 (NIV2011)*

Check yourself. Right now, start noticing how you think and how you speak. What are you putting after God's Name of "I AM?"

Chapter 6

Speaking As One

*G*od used His Name when speaking through Jesus. I have capitalized God's Name in the following scriptures.

Jesus told them, "I AM the bread of life.
Whoever comes to me will never become hungry,
and whoever believes in me will never become thirsty."
John 6:35 (GW)

"I AM the bread of life."
John 6:48 (GW)

Jesus spoke to the Pharisees again. He said,
"I AM the light of the world.
Whoever follows me will have a life filled with light
and will never live in the dark."
John 8:12 (GW)

"While I AM in the world, I AM the light of the world."
John 9:5 (NIV2011)

"Very truly I tell you," Jesus answered,
"before Abraham was born, I AM!"
John 8:58 (NIV2011)

"I AM the gate.
Those who enter the sheep pen through me will be saved.
They will go in and out of the sheep pen and find food."
John 10:9 (GW)

"I AM the good shepherd.
The good shepherd gives his life for the sheep."
John 10:11 (GW)

Jesus said to her,
"I AM the one who brings people back to life, and I AM life itself.
Those who believe in me will live even if they die."
John 11:25 (GW)

Jesus answered him,
"I AM the way, the truth, and the life.
No one goes to the Father except through me."
John 14:6 (GW)

"I AM the true vine, and my Father is the gardener."
John 15:1 (NIV2011)

In the Revelation given to John, Jesus spoke again, using God's Name first.

"I AM the Alpha and the Omega," says the Lord God,
"who is, and who was, and who is to come,
the Almighty."
Revelation 1:8 (NIV2011)

When I saw him, I fell at his feet as though dead.
Then he placed his right hand on me and said:
"Do not be afraid.
I AM the First and the Last.
I AM the Living One;
I was dead, and now look, I AM alive for ever and ever!
And I hold the keys of death and Hades."
Revelation 1:17-18 (NIV2011)

He said to me: "It is done.
I AM the Alpha and the Omega, the Beginning and the End.
To the thirsty I will give water without cost
from the spring of the water of life.
Those who are victorious will inherit all this,
and I will be their God and they will be my children."
Revelation 21:6-7 (NIV2011)

"I AM the Alpha and the Omega,
the First and the Last, the Beginning and the End."
Revelation 22:13 (NIV2011)

Isaiah, the prophet, who was on earth long after God created the world and long before Jesus, spoke God's Words that confirm what He spoke through Jesus.

"This is what the LORD says—
Israel's King and Redeemer, the LORD Almighty:
I AM the first and I AM the last;
apart from me there is no God."
Isaiah 44:6 (NIV2011)

"Listen to me, Jacob,
Israel, whom I have called:
I AM he;
I AM the first and I AM the last."
Isaiah 48:12 (NIV2011)

Chapter 7

Knowing The One

*W*e may not have thought about God's Name as much as we have thought about The Name of Jesus. Many of us learned at a young age to end our prayers with the phrase, "In Jesus' Name." Didn't Jesus say …

> *"I will do anything you ask {the Father} in my name so*
> *that the Father will be given glory because of the Son."*
> *John 14:13 (GW)*

If that is all we read, it sounds like a surefire formula. Pray and ask for anything we want in the Name of Jesus. That sounds like a blank check.

We can think of many people who have prayed in the Name of Jesus and it appeared there were positive results. Jesus spoke about some of those people.

It appeared they had worked for Jesus. So imagine their surprise when they died and discovered they were not going to heaven. I can imagine them, standing at The Pearly Gates, reciting over and over again … "In Jesus' Name … in Jesus' Name." And each time the gates did not swing open, their cries became louder. "In Jesus' Name!!!!"

What happened next is scary to think about. Here is what Jesus had to say about them.

> *"Not everyone who says to me,*
> *'Lord, Lord!' will enter the kingdom of heaven,*
> *but only the person who does what my Father in heaven wants.*
> *Many will say to me on that day,*
> *'Lord, Lord, didn't we prophesy in your name?*
> *Didn't we force out demons*
> *and do many miracles by the power and authority of your name?'*
> *Then I will tell them publicly,*
> *'I've never known you. Get away from me, you evil people.'"*
> *Matthew 7:21-23 (GW)*

Why would using Jesus' Name not open the Gates to Heaven? Why would it not guarantee us eternal life? In His Conversation with God, Jesus clearly defined what eternal life means and how we can enter into eternal life.

> *This is eternal life:*
> *to know you, the only true God,*
> *and Jesus Christ, whom you sent.*
> *John 17:3 (GW)*

The real Key to The Kingdom is truly knowing The One. "Knowing" is very different from "knowing about." Knowing about The One may let you imitate the right words, like a password. Knowing The One is about a True Love Relationship, as Jesus described it.

> *"However, I want the world to know that I love the Father*
> *and that I am doing exactly what the Father*
> *has commanded me to do. ..."*
> *John 14:31 (GW)*

> *"If you love me, you will obey my commandments."*
> *John 14:15 (GW)*

What does it mean to know The One? Meditate on Jesus' Words and consider your relationship with The One—God, Jesus and The Holy Spirit. Do you love Him and know Him so well, that people around you see Him in you? Would He welcome you into eternal life or would He say sadly, "I never knew you."

Notice in these scripture verses how all Three Parts of The One are working together. Also notice how they want us to be aware we are a part of them and they of us.

> *Jesus answered, "I am the way and the truth and the life.*
> *No one comes to the Father except through me.*
> *If you really know me, you will know my Father as well.*
> *From now on, you do know him and have seen him."*
>
> *Phillip said, "Lord, show us the Father*
> *and that will be enough for us."*
>
> *Jesus answered: "Don't you know me, Philip,*
> *even after I have been among you such a long time?*
> *Anyone who has seen me has seen the Father.*
> *How can you say, 'Show us the Father'?*
>
> *Don't you believe that I am in the Father, and that the Father is in me?*
> *The words I say to you I do not speak on my own authority.*
> *Rather, it is the Father, living in me, who is doing his work.*
>
> *Believe me when I say that I am in the Father and the Father is in me;*
> *or at least believe on the evidence of the works themselves.*
> *Very truly I tell you, whoever believes in me*
> *will do the works I have been doing,*
> *and they will do even greater things than these,*

because I am going to the Father.
And I will do whatever you ask in my name,
so that the Father may be glorified in the Son.
You may ask me for anything in my name, and I will do it.

If you love me, keep my commands.
And I will ask the Father,
and he will give you another advocate
to help you and be with you forever—the Spirit of truth.
The world cannot accept him,
because it neither sees him nor knows him.
But you know him, for he lives with you and will be in you.
I will not leave you as orphans; I will come to you.

Before long, the world will not see me anymore, but you will see me.
Because I live, you also will live.
On that day you will realize that I am in my Father,
and you are in me, and I am in you.
Whoever has my commands and keeps them is the one who loves me.
The one who loves me will be loved by my Father,
and I too will love them and show myself to them."
John 14:6-21 (NIV2011)

When we truly know the One, what we ask in His Name will be what He would desire. Actually we will no longer need to ask. We will simply agree with God, Jesus and The Holy Spirit. Perhaps we should end our prayers with All Three of Their Names.

Father God, I AM coming to You in the Power of Your Word, Jesus, Your Word made flesh and now abiding with You and Your Precious Holy Spirit, Who is bringing Your Words to my memory. I thank you that All of You live in me and I live in You! Amen!

Chapter 8

Power In The Name of Jesus, The Word!

How is it possible that those who did great miracles in the Name of Jesus would not be going to heaven?

How is it possible that in our present day, we see true miracles of God, that seem to happen through people who have glaring sins in their life?

The Power of God cannot be stopped, even when it flows through a weak vessel. God seemed to have delighted in sending His Word through struggling Christians. We can take some comfort in knowing God can work through us, even when our lives don't match His Words at all times.

When the Name of Jesus is used, His identification as The Word of God comes to the forefront.

Remember Jesus was identified as The Word.

In the beginning the Word already existed.
The Word was with God,
and the Word was God.
John 1:1 (GW)

149

The Word became human and lived among us.
We saw his glory. It was the glory
that the Father shares with his only Son,
a glory full of kindness and truth.
John 1:14 (GW)

God's Word has a Power all its own.

God's word is living and active. It is sharper than any two-edged sword
and cuts as deep as the place where soul and spirit meet,
the place where joints and marrow meet.
God's word judges a person's thoughts and intentions.
Hebrews 4:12 (GW)

God's Word will accomplish the Purpose for which He sent it.

As the rain and the snow come down from heaven,
and do not return to it without watering the earth
and making it bud and flourish,
so that it yields seed for the sower and bread for the eater,
so is my word that goes out from my mouth:
it will not return to me empty,
but will accomplish what I desire
and achieve the purpose for which I sent it.
Isaiah 55:10-11 (NIV2011)

No one, not even satan, can make The Word of God invalid. If the True Word of God is used, it will stand forever!

"Grass dries up, and flowers wither,
but the word of our God will last forever."
Isaiah 40:8 (GW)

The person who delivers The Word has the first opportunity to benefit from it. But if he does not receive The Word, he is simply a delivery person.

Can The Word of God ever be used wrongly? Unfortunately, yes. Remember satan can quote scripture. He did just that when He tempted Jesus. However, satan used the scriptures followed by his own spin. He was attempting to use the same tactics with Jesus that he had used with Eve. He quoted scripture out of context and used it to attempt to confuse, not clarify.

Jesus also quoted scripture, but He used The Word of God rightly. When we read The Word of God, we should ask The Holy Spirit to clarify for us what it means for us at that moment. We should also read scriptures in context. Sometimes not reading the whole passage of scripture can change the entire meaning.

Consider the plight of the poor man who felt suicidal. He grabbed his Bible in desperation, seeking direction. Apparently he did not ask The Holy Spirit for clear direction. He was just looking for a "quick fix." Satan, of course, was only too willing to help him.

Opening his Bible at random, the man read about Judas.

> *... then he went away and hanged himself.*
> *Matthew 27:5 (NIV2011)*

That did not sound encouraging. So the man tried again. This time he read

> *..."Go and do likewise."*
> *Luke 10:37 (NIV2011)*

We don't know the end of that story. But it illustrates well how satan loves to get in the middle of scripture and entice us to misunderstand it. Satan can work through the actions of humans who freely interpret the scriptures, as they see it.

In addition to asking The Holy Spirit to interpret The Word for us, we should also ask the same for others. We can pray and share the Words God gives us. Then we can be at peace, knowing The Word will achieve The Purpose for which God sent it.

Now let's go back to those people who used God's Word to prophesy, cast out demons and do miracles. Yet, Jesus said He never knew them. Were they doing magic or did the miracles really occur from God?

So I want you to know
that no one speaking by God's Spirit says,
"Jesus is cursed."
No one can say, "Jesus is Lord,"
except by the Holy Spirit.
1 Corinthians 12:3 (GW)

Can a Word of God pass our tongues and not do us good? Doesn't the water wet the inside of the glass? Yes, The Word of God coming through us does us good, but we must believe The Word is for us as well as for those to whom we are speaking. We must ask The Holy Spirit to reveal to us what The Words we are sharing mean for us in this time. And we must live The Words God is allowing us to share.

Many people have delivered a Word of God spoken to Moses or David or Paul, but they did not believe that Word was for people today, including themselves. Those who do believe and receive it will be blessed. Those who hear, but do not believe and receive will not have The Life offered to them. That includes the one who spoke The Word.

Jesus told a parable about planting and reaping.

"The farmer plants the word.
Some people are like seeds that were planted along the road.
Whenever they hear the word, Satan comes at once

152

and takes away the word that was planted in them.
Other people are like seeds that were planted on rocky ground.
Whenever they hear the word, they accept it at once with joy.
But they don't develop any roots. They last for a short time.
When suffering or persecution comes along because of the word,
they immediately fall {from faith}.

Other people are like seeds planted among thornbushes.
They hear the word, but the worries of life, the deceitful pleasures of riches,
and the desires for other things take over.
They choke the word so that it can't produce anything.

Others are like seeds planted on good ground.
They hear the word, accept it, and produce crops—
thirty, sixty, or one hundred times as much as was planted."
Mark 4:14-20 (GW)

There is Power in the Name of Jesus! There is Power in The Word of God! That Power comes to Life in those who hear the Word, accept it and allow God to do what is necessary to produce a bountiful crop. Remember God is The Gardener!

(Jesus speaking)
"I am the true vine, and
my Father is the gardener."
John 15:1 (NIV2011)

Life
In The Womb!

Jesus replied,
"Very truly I tell you,
no one can see the kingdom of God
unless they are born again."
John 3:3 (NIV2011)

"On that day, you will realize that
I AM in my Father,
and you are in me, and
I AM in you."
John 14:20 (NIV2011)

Chapter 1

Together Constantly!

*J*esus gave us a picture of how seeds can grow and produce a bountiful harvest. We love the harvest, but we often don't think much about what is happening in the time between when the seed is planted and when we get to see the evidence of it.

We have discussed the Celebration of True Love in which God can bring together the seeds of Life from a man and a woman. With God's nurturing, new life will ultimately be revealed to us when the baby is born.

Everything God did, as revealed through Jesus, was a revelation of The True Gift God wants to give us. Many of us look at the Life of Jesus and try to imitate Him. We have the mistaken notion if we could just follow Jesus, step for step, we would somehow turn out to be just like Him.

But no matter how hard we try, the person staring back at us from the mirror does not seem like God, Jesus or The Holy Spirit. If we heed Jesus' Words, we can easily end up in a performance crisis. What does He expect of us?

"Be perfect, therefore,
as your heavenly Father is perfect."
Matthew 5:48 (NIV2011)

How can that be? He would have to be closer than just walking with us. He would have to be inside of us … or we'd have to be inside Him. Many of us connect with God on what we call a regular basis. But regular contact is not the same as constant contact.

Jesus demonstrated for us from the beginning the kind of relationship He had with His Father. Even though the Father, Son and The Holy Spirit are One, sometimes it is helpful to see each part to understand how They fit together into The Whole.

Jesus stayed in the womb for the same amount of time as other babies. There was no indication He was delivered early. He stayed in the womb, growing physically toward the day when He would exit the womb, mature enough to function in the larger world.

Even after Jesus exited Mary's physical womb, He stayed in the Spiritual Womb with The Father. Jesus frequently talked about things His listeners knew about in their physical world. He then used what they knew of the physical world to explain how things worked in the Spiritual World. The Spiritual World is often similar to the physical world, but not always identical.

Many people denote human male traits to God because we so often talk about "Him," as if He is male. When He came as Jesus, He came as a man. However, God is far beyond the limitations of human gender design. So we can speak of God in a figurative way, as having a "womb." The relationship between Jesus and His Father was a "mutual womb relationship." Listen again to how Jesus described it.

"… I am in the Father
and the Father is in me.
The words I say to you I do not speak on my own authority.
Rather, it is the Father, living in me, who is doing his work."
John 14:10 (NIV2011)

"I and the Father are one."
John 10:30 (NIV2011)

"I have not spoken on my own.
Instead, the Father who sent me told me what I should say
and how I should say it.
I know that what he commands is eternal life.
Whatever I say is what the Father told me to say."
John 12:49-50 (GW)

Like a baby in the womb, Jesus was in constant contact with His Father. He received all His Spiritual Nourishment from the Father. He shared His Very Life at every moment with His Father. What came out of His Mouth was just what the Father had given Him to say. It is this womb relationship that truly made them One.

Jesus even taught about being in the womb.

Once there was a man named Nicodemus, who acknowledged Jesus was a teacher sent by God. He came to this conclusion, not because of any relationship with Jesus, but because of the miracles he had seen Jesus perform.

Jesus then told him The True Secret of the Kingdom. It is the same "Secret" that Christians frequently talk about—being "born again."

Jesus replied,
"Very truly I tell you,
no one can see the kingdom of God
unless they are born again."
John 3:3 (NIV2011)

If you are a Christian, it is likely you have used the expression, "born again," to denote your connection with Jesus. Before reading any further, stop and think about what you believe being a "born again Christian" means.

Nicodemus was very literal. He just didn't see how such a preposterous thing could possibly be.

"How can someone be born when they are old?"
Nicodemus asked.
"Surely they cannot enter a second time into their mother's womb
to be born!"
John 3:4 (NIV2011)

Jesus continued with His Explanation.

Jesus answered,
"Very truly I tell you,
no one can enter the kingdom of God
unless they are born of water and the Spirit.
Flesh gives birth to flesh, but the Spirit gives birth to spirit."
John 3:5-6 (NIV2011)

Let's look at what Jesus said in the style He usually taught. He taught about something physical. Then He linked it to something spiritual.

Let's look at the physical environment of the womb where babies grow before they are born.

Chapter 2

Womb Living

*J*n fact, babies are born of water. Consider the following amazing facts about amniotic fluid. Amniotic fluid is the fluid that surrounds the growing baby in the womb.

This mostly water-like fluid originates from the mother's own blood. Again, God has given us a physical picture of that which is important spiritually.

> *And there are three that bear witness on earth:*
> *the Spirit, the water, and the blood;*
> *and these three agree as one.*
> *1 John 5:8 (NKJV)*

The Spirit, the water and the blood all work together with the same goal of taking care of the baby.

At first, amniotic fluid is mainly water with electrolytes, but by about the 12-14th week, the liquid also contains proteins, carbohydrates, lipids and phospholipids, and urea, all of which aid in the growth of the baby.

The amniotic fluid fulfills important functions for the baby. It is inhaled and exhaled by the baby. It is essential that fluid be breathed into the lungs in order for them to develop normally. Swallowed amniotic fluid also creates urine and contributes to the formation of meconium (early form of stool).

Amniotic fluid protects the developing baby by cushioning against blows to the mother's abdomen. The fluid allows the baby to move inside the womb and thus develop its musculoskeletal system. Amniotic fluid swallowed by the baby helps in the formation of the gastrointestinal tract.[1]

The water provided by God in the womb is truly Living Water!

Inside the mother, the tiny baby is growing. He is nourished. He is being prepared to breathe in the outside environment he will soon experience. His wastes are taken away. The baby is completely cared for, even as it is developing a glorious new body.

The baby is protected. It is well documented that babies in the womb can hear what happens outside the mother's body. They are not completely separated from the world. But they are in a protected environment. Most importantly, they are close enough to hear their mother's heartbeat.

Babies don't jump in the womb one moment and out of the womb into the world the next. They stay in the womb. They abide, in a God designed Connection with their mother.

The baby is dependent upon the mother for everything. It has no need to seek anything beyond its borders. It is in its own form of The Garden of Eden, where provision is complete and faithfully delivered. The baby is learning important lessons of life. He learns how to stay connected to His Life Giver. He learns how to receive and enjoy what he receives.

This, then, is what it is like to be in the womb of God. Unlike the baby, in its physical Garden of Eden, spiritually, we run in and out of the womb. When we start feeling a little cramped in the womb, we kick our way out. When the world seems to have too many troubles, we want to go to the womb, to take a break.

Sometimes when things get really rough, we might dream of a world where everything is peaceful and good. We may think we are dreaming of a future Heaven. In reality, we are remembering the Heaven we once had, and could have again, if we stayed in God's Womb.

We use phrases like "born again," but we really don't take the time to remember what it was like when we were waiting to be born the first time. Even if we did, we would probably be asking the same question Nicodemus asked. How could we ever get back in the womb again?

Jesus spoke of the significant physical element of being born of the water. But He also said it was essential we be born of The Spirit. To allow our Spirit to grow, we must abide. We must stay in constant connection and unity with the only One Who can truly nourish us, protect us, and take our sins (our wastes) away. God desires that we spend all our time nestled right next to His Heart, while He gives us room to grow and flex our spiritual muscles.

As recorded in The Gospel of John, Chapter 15, Jesus gave the same directive multiple times. (Underline added for emphasis)

"Remain in me, as I also remain in you.
No branch can bear fruit by itself; it must remain in the vine.
Neither can you bear fruit unless you remain in me."
John 15:4 (NIV2011)

" … If you remain in me and I in you, you will bear much fruit;
apart from me you can do nothing.
If you do not remain in me,
you are like a branch that is thrown away and withers;
such branches are picked up, thrown into the fire and burned.
If you remain in me and my words remain in you,

ask whatever you wish, and it will be done for you."
John 15:5-7 (NIV2011)

"As the Father has loved me, so have I loved you.
Now <u>remain in my love.</u>
If you keep my commands, you will <u>remain in my love</u>,
just as I have kept my Father's commands
and <u>remain in his love</u>."
John 15:9-10 (NIV2011)

God could have appeared as Jesus in any number of His Creative Ways. But He chose to start Jesus' visible Life on earth by coming through the womb of Mary. Jesus stayed in Mary's womb and grew.

There is one more important thing to know about womb living. How does the growing baby maintain its connection to its Source of Life? God created an amazing connector called The Umbilical Cord.

1. "Amniotic fluid." *Wikipedia: The Free Encyclopedia*. Wikimedia Foundation, Inc. 9 February 2015. Web. 21 February 2015. <https://en.wikipedia.org/wiki/Amniotic_fluid>

Chapter 3

The True Vine

$\mathcal{T}$he umbilical cord is the connector between the mother and the developing baby.

The cord carries oxygen rich blood to the baby. This is especially important because the baby is unable to breathe (having neither functioning lungs nor an oxygen source) and the cord provides the baby the oxygen it needs to live.

The umbilical cord also serves as a source of nutrients, providing calories, proteins and fats, as well as vitamins and nutrients for the baby.

Blood that is no longer oxygenated and the blood through the cord to the mother, whose own blood circulation processes the baby's wastes and eliminates it, carries waste products from the baby.

Cord blood, which can be extracted after the baby has been born, is rich in stem cells that can be used to treat many blood and immunological disorders, as well as some cancers.[1]

These are all things that happen in the physical world of the womb. However, look at how closely they line up with the spiritual world of The Womb of God.

The umbilical cord that connects mother and child looks very much like a vine. Jesus is our Connector to the other parts of The Blessed Trinity. Jesus identified Himself as The Vine and us as the Branches.

"I am the vine. You are the branches.
Those who live in me while I live in them will produce a lot of fruit.
But you can't produce anything without me."
John 15:5 (GW)

If we cut the Spiritual Cord and try to do life on our own, we will immediately discover what "nothing" means. Deprived of Life and breath, starved, overflowing with sins that can never be taken away, and no hope of healing is exactly what satan would want for us. But it is the opposite of what God wants. He wants us to have Life and have it to the fullest! Jesus said:

" ...I have come that they may have life,
and have it to the full."
John 10:10 (NIV2011)

How do we get Life to the full? Don't cut the cord! Abide in the Womb of God and let Him feed you on the Word of God.

We might think we can just float in God's Womb and everything will be nice and peaceful. However, that is not entirely true.

According to William G. T. Shedd, a nineteenth-century theologian, "A ship in harbor is safe, but that is not what ships are built for." The initial womb is a place to grow, but when we grow beyond the bounds of that womb, we are pushed out into the world. It can be rough out there. How smooth the sailing is depends in large measure upon our choices.

Actually God begins His Demonstration of Choice in the physical womb. Let's look at an important organ of choice called the placenta. It only exists for the

166

time the baby is in the womb. It is created specifically for a time and a purpose. You also were created for a time and a purpose.

Let's look closer at the interesting placenta.

1. Cloe, Adam. "What Are the 3 Functions of the Umbilical Cord?" *eHow*. Demand Media. n.d. Web. 20 April 2015. <http://www.ehow.com/about_4672809_what-functions-umbilical-cord.html>

Chapter 4

The Blood Filter

*W*e looked at the importance of the umbilical cord, which carries blood back and forth between the mother and baby. We might think the mother and baby share the same blood. But they do not.

The placenta is a temporary organ connected to the baby by the umbilical cord. It is made of blood vessels and connective tissue. It has two parts, one of which is genetically and biologically part of the baby, the other part of the mother.

The mother's and baby's blood never mix. The placenta acts as an exchange surface between the mother and baby. Nutrients and oxygen are passed over by diffusion.

Remember the baby results from the genes of both father and mother. So the baby is not just a copy of the mother. The baby may have a different blood type from that of the mother. If the blood from the mother is mixed with the blood of the baby, and their blood types are not compatible, both could become ill and even die.

The placenta acts as a protective filter. It filters out some substances that come from the mother, which could harm the fetus. However, many other substances are not filtered out, including alcohol and some chemicals associated with smoking cigarettes.

Just as God partnered with Adam and Eve, so He partners with us. Some things that happen inside of our body are totally under God's Control. We cannot control them at all. However, some things we do control.

We see the partnership between God and a human mother through the functioning of the placenta. God, through the placenta, mercifully keeps some harmful things away from the baby. However, God does not keep everything away from the baby. Part of what reaches the baby depends on the choice of the mother. If a pregnant mother drinks alcohol, the placental barrier will not stop it from affecting the baby. It is important that the mother make good choices.[1]

God protects us spiritually from many of the evil things in life. But some things God leaves for us to decide. He guides us. He makes it clear what is good and what is evil. But, as He did from the beginning of time, He allows His Humans to make choices that will affect their Life eternally.

> *…I have set before you life and death, blessings and curses.*
> *Now choose life,*
> *so that you and your children may live*
> *and that you may love the LORD your God,*
> *listen to his voice,*
> *and hold fast to him.*
> *For the LORD is your life …*
> *Deuteronomy 30:19-20 (NIV2011)*

1. "Placenta." *Wikipedia: The Free Encyclopedia*. Wikimedia Foundation, Inc. 2 March 2014. Web. 29 April 2015.
   < https://simple.wikipedia.org/w/index.php?title=Placenta&oldid=4741870>

Jesus — God With Us!

*"The virgin will conceive
and give birth to a son,
and they will call him Immanuel.
(which means "God with us").
Matthew 1:23 (NIV2011)*

*"She will give birth to a son,
and you are to give him the name Jesus,
because he will save his people
from their sins."
Matthew 1:21 (NIV2011)*

Chapter 1

Saved From What?

*M*any of us proudly tell others we are "saved." Yet, when the non-believer presses us to say exactly what it is we are saved from, we may have a hard time explaining it.

The First Chapter of Matthew's Gospel, Verse 23, records Jesus' other name of Immanuel and verifies Who He is. Immanuel means "God with us."

The First Chapter of Matthew's Gospel, Verse 21, verifies Jesus' Mission. He came to save His People from their sins.

What is sin? Sin is anything that keeps us from receiving all God wants to give us.

Who are His People? It is true Jesus' Message was first preached to the Jews. However, it was never His Intention that His Words just remain with one group of people. His Message was for all. He came to save everyone.

> *... He doesn't want to destroy <u>anyone</u>*
> *but wants <u>all people</u> to have an opportunity to turn to him*
> *and change the way they think and act.*
> *2 Peter 3:9 (GW)*
> (Underline added for emphasis)

When Jesus healed, who did He heal?

> *... And great multitudes followed Him,*
> *and He healed them <u>all</u>.*
> *Matthew 12:15 (NKJV)*
> (Underline added for emphasis)

From what did Jesus come to save us? There is no getting around it. He came to save us from sin.

The word, "sin" is mentioned over 400 times in the Bible (depending on which translation is used). Most of us hate to think about sin. For many of us, the word, "sin," brings up visions of times we were "bad." The remembrance of sins reminds us of how hard it is for us not to sin. We want to do right, and yet ... we slip back so easily.

Take heart. Even Paul, who was a great missionary, struggled with sin. Paul was willing to help others by admitting he was locked into the same struggle his listeners were having.

> *So I've discovered this truth:*
> *Evil is present with me*
> *even when I want to do what God's standards say is good.*
> *I take pleasure in God's standards in my inner being.*
> *However, I see a different standard {at work} throughout my body.*
> *It is at war with the standards my mind sets*
> *and tries to take me captive to sin's standards*
> *which still exist throughout my body.*
> *What a miserable person I am!*
> *Who will rescue me from my dying body?*
> *I thank God that our Lord Jesus Christ rescues me! ...*
> *Romans 7:21-25 (GW)*

When we put the "I AM" principle into place, we see part of the problem in Paul's statement. When we say what we believe about ourselves and tag on God's Name (I AM) after it, it sounds like we are in bad shape.

What a miserable person I AM! ...
Romans 7:24 (GW)

But into that misery comes Jesus, who puts His Father's Name into the right place—First! Look up and see what He is offering us. These are some of the things from which He saves us.

He saves us from Hunger and Thirst.
Jesus told them, "I AM the bread of life.
Whoever comes to me will never become hungry,
and whoever believes in me will never become thirsty."
John 6:35 (GW)

He saves us from Darkness.
When Jesus spoke again to the people, he said,
"I AM the light of the world.
Whoever follows me will never walk in darkness,
but will have the light of life."
John 8:12 (NIV2011)

He saves us from being fenced in.
"I AM the gate.
Those who enter the sheep pen through me will be saved.
They will go in and out of the sheep pen and find food."
John 10:9 (GW)

He saves us from harm.

"I AM the good shepherd.
The good shepherd gives his life for the sheep."
John 10:11 (GW)

He saves us from death.

Jesus said to her, "I AM the one who brings people back to life,
and I AM life itself. Those who believe in me will live even if they die."
John 11:25 (GW)

He saves us from deception and death.

Jesus answered him, "I AM the way, the truth, and the life.
No one goes to the Father except through me."
John 14:6 (GW)

He saves us from being cut off from The Source of Life.

"I AM the true vine, and my Father is the gardener."
John 15:1 (NIV2011)

He saves us from the limits of one Time.

"I AM the Alpha and the Omega," says the Lord God,
"who is, and who was, and who is to come,
the Almighty."
Revelation 1:8 (NIV2011)

He saves us from an eternity of Hell.

When I saw him, I fell at his feet as though dead.
Then he placed his right hand on me and said:
"Do not be afraid.
I AM the First and the Last.
I AM the Living One;
I was dead, and now look, I AM alive for ever and ever!
And I hold the keys of death and Hades."
Revelation 1:17-18 (NIV2011)

When we can't keep ourselves from being pulled back into sin, we begin to fear punishment for our sins by death. Death to many is the absolutely worst thing that can happen to a person. Why?

Death seems to make people disappear. We are not completely certain where they went. We hope they went to a beautiful place and are having a great time. We hope to see them in that place some time in the future.

But there is that business of hell. What if they went to hell? What if we were wrong about everything and we are headed there? We need more time to clean up our act. We don't want to die yet. We are afraid.

If you want the quick, short answer of why Jesus came, here it is. He came to save everyone from sin and from their number one enemy—death. He came to wipe out the fear of death.

> *Since all of these sons and daughters have flesh and blood,*
> *Jesus took on flesh and blood to be like them.*
> *He did this so that by dying he would destroy the one*
> *who had power over death (that is, the devil).*
> *In this way he would free those who were slaves*
> *all their lives because they were afraid of dying.*
> *Hebrews 2:14-15 (GW)*

> *The last enemy to be destroyed is death.*
> *1 Corinthians 15:26 (NIV2011)*

Jesus fully demonstrated to everyone He was, in fact, dead. His physical body was mangled beyond recognition. Then it was verified by multiple people he had died. His Body was wrapped up and placed in a secured tomb. Satan seemed to have had perfect opportunity to say, "Yes, I won! Be afraid … be very afraid of dying. You can see it's not a pretty picture. You will suffer and then you are all mine. God's not coming for you. You sinned."

Jesus was said to be human, He was God. So, of course, He didn't sin. Wouldn't you have to be God not to sin? We can't be God. Satan proved that too.

Paul says, we are doomed to constantly deal with evil that is going to pull on us. What can we do?

How do we deal with the sin problem?

Chapter 2

Would God Forsake Us?

*S*atan would like us to believe our sins separate us from God. But it is not possible for us to be separated from God's Love.

When we sin, God does not leave us or turn away from looking at us. He always sees us. But sin will get in the way of our seeing Him, hearing Him, feeling His Touch and receiving what He has for us. God is very present, but when we are loaded down with sins, we can't see past them to see that God is there.

> *Surely the arm of the LORD is not too short to save,*
> *nor his ear too dull to hear.*
> *But your iniquities have separated you from your God;*
> *your sins have hidden his face from you …*
> *Isaiah 59:1-2 (NIV2011)*

Be sure to note that sins did not sever our relationship with God, but they hid His Face from us.

Many puzzle over Jesus' statement from the cross that seems to imply God abandoned Him when He took on all the sins of the world. Many even equate the darkness that came over the land as a sure sign that God simply looked away from Jesus.

From noon until three in the afternoon
darkness came over all the land.
About three in the afternoon Jesus cried out in a loud voice,
"Eli, Eli, lema sabachthani?"
(which means "My God, my God, why have you forsaken me?").
Matthew 27:45-46 (NIV2011)

Satan loves to quote this verse. But remember who he is. Jesus called satan the "father of lies."

God, Jesus and The Holy Spirit have been together forever, and forever they shall be. It is impossible for them to be separated. They were all together at the cross.

Jesus was so sure that God was still a part of Him that He called Him twice, "<u>My</u> God." Jesus was so sure of His Father's Goodness and Provision that He continued to suffer without asking anything.

Did Jesus suffer in the way a human would suffer in such a circumstance? Yes. God and The Holy Spirit were One with Jesus. However, on that day, Jesus, in the body of a human, took center stage.

We have a chief priest who is able to sympathize with our weaknesses.
He was tempted in every way that we are, but he didn't sin.
Hebrews 4:15 (GW)

Remember what we learned in an early chapter. Because God, Jesus and The Holy Spirit are One, what they say in unison is for our benefit.

Because Jesus experienced temptation when he suffered,
he is able to help others when they are tempted.
Hebrews 2:18 (GW)

Jesus wanted us to know how it would be for us if we were weighted down with even a fraction of what He was experiencing. It would be dark. As the darkness continued, and sins piled up even more, it would seem God was not there. We might even start to question whether He had ever been our Father.

Jesus wanted us to know that would be a vulnerable time when we would need to remember who we are. When satan tempted Jesus in the desert, he came at him again and again, questioning who He was, by saying, "If you are The Son of God." Jesus knew who He was then, and He knew Who He was on the cross.

In the darkness of sin, we need to cry out to our Father in faith. It is ok to ask Him if He is there. He will answer.

"…I will not leave you nor forsake you."
Joshua 1:5 (NKJV)

When Jesus seemed to question if God had forsaken Him, He was speaking for all who were loaded down with sin.

But Jesus knew He had not been forsaken. When Jesus said, "It is finished", God removed all sin from Him. And Jesus released His Spirit.

Jesus saw God and The Holy Spirit waiting to celebrate Their Completeness with Him. When we surrender our sins and release ourselves to the care of The One, we will see Them waiting to celebrate with us.

Chapter 3

Never Alone

*J*s there a way to get rid of sin and reset the clock, so to speak? Yes, there is. Step One for sin removal is recognizing that we can never get rid of sin by ourselves and we can never stay free in our own strength. We will need the ongoing deep cleaning only God can give. Instead of running away from God, we can run to Him. Be advised—satan will not like this.

Satan would have us believe that when we sin, we are "bad." Satan would like us to believe God won't tolerate sin and therefore, won't tolerate us. Satan would like us to believe we can't go to God and God won't come to us. But God, in fact, did and does come to us!

> *For God so loved the world that he gave his one and only Son,*
> *that whoever believes in him shall not perish*
> *but have eternal life.*
> *For God did not send his Son into the world to condemn the world,*
> *but to save the world through him.*
> *John 3:16-17 (NIV2011)*

There is nothing that can ever separate us from God and His Love for us. Our bodies are The Temple of The Holy Spirit. God was within us before we ever knew He was there. He is not going to leave His Temple because we came in with the mud of the outside world on our feet. No matter how many times satan knocks on the door of God's Temple, God is not leaving!

Let's look at two writers who discovered the Profound Truth that we can never be separated from God's Love. The writings of David the Psalmist are recorded in the Old Testament. The writings of Paul are recorded in the New Testament.

Read all the way through Psalm, Chapter 139. Verses 7 through 12 of David's Words are quoted here.

Where can I go from your Spirit?
Where can I flee from your presence?
If I go up to the heavens, you are there;
If I make my bed in the depths, you are there.
If I rise on the wings of the dawn,
if I settle on the far side of the sea,
even there your hand will guide me,
your right hand will hold me fast.
If I say, "Surely the darkness will hide me
and the light become night around me,"
even the darkness will not be dark to you;
the night will shine like the day,
for darkness is as light to you.
Psalm 139:7-12 (NIV2011)

For I am convinced
that neither death nor life,
neither angels nor demons,
neither the present nor the future, nor any powers,
neither height nor depth,
nor anything else in all creation,
will be able to separate us from the love of God
that is in Christ Jesus our Lord.
Romans 8:38-39 (NIV2011)

Chapter 4

Repent!

Satan would prefer we never connect with God. But if we do, he has various ways of trying to defuse what he sees as a bomb on his desired kingdom. The first is to encourage us to just let God pull a few weeds instead of replanting the whole garden.

Many times when we are caught in the midst of sin, we are sorry. But all too often we are just sorry we got caught or we are sorry about the consequences of our sin instead of being truly sorry for the sin itself.

Sometimes it feels good to get the top layer of sin removed, but we'd rather wait until another time to go any further. If we leave any seeds of wickedness for satan, he will have a head start on causing future trouble.

So when we detect a problem, the best thing we can do is run to God immediately and ask him in all humility to reveal to us what He sees in us.

Examine me, O God, and know my mind.
Test me, and know my thoughts.
See whether I am on an evil path.
Then lead me on the everlasting path.
Psalm 139:23-24 (GW)

Repenting begins with humility, praying and seeking God's Face.

If my people, who are called by my name,
will humble themselves and pray and seek my face
and turn from their wicked ways,
then I will hear from heaven,
and I will forgive their sin
and will heal their land.
2 Chronicles 7:14 (NIV2011)

Sometimes we are overwhelmed when God's Light shines in our darkness. We have the urge to ask Him to turn down The Light when we see what has been hiding within us. However, we can rest assured that nothing we have to release to God is too much for Him to handle.

Whoever covers over his sins does not prosper.
Whoever confesses and abandons them receives compassion.
Proverbs 28:13 (GW)

God is faithful and reliable. If we confess our sins,
he forgives them and cleanses us from everything we've done wrong.
1 John 1:9 (GW)

There is that word again—ALL. When we are truly repentant, God will forgive and forget. Often we say we forgive, but we do not forget. The first time we slip up or someone we have forgiven slips up, we are quick to say, "This is just like all the other times this has happened." However, if we were truly forgetting, as God does, the offense would be the first time we ever remember it happening!

"I alone am the one
who is going to wipe away your rebellious actions for my own sake.
I will not remember your sins {anymore}."
Isaiah 43:25 (GW)

To truly repent is to turn from our wicked ways. That means to go another way entirely. Having been made aware of our sin and having confessed it to God and having received His Forgiveness, we can begin again.

Be aware that satan would like you to remember your sin in detail. He can more easily convince you that you are not a new person, if he can keep you giving "your testimony" about the "bad old days." Give satan no credit for how far down you once were. Testify only to the new person in Christ you are today!

When Jesus forgave the sin of the woman taken in adultery, he told her to go and sin no more. He says the same to us. He wants us to walk away free and not look back!

> *"So if the Son sets you free, you will be absolutely free."*
> *John 8:36 (GW)*

Chapter 5

The Unforgivable Sin

*T*here is a scripture that worries many people. Jesus says there is one unforgivable sin. Satan pops up immediately, and shouts, "Yeah, and you committed it!" Let's look a little closer at what Jesus said.

(Jesus speaking)
"So I can guarantee that people will be forgiven for any sin or cursing.
However, cursing the Spirit will not be forgiven.
Whoever speaks a word against the Son of Man will be forgiven.
But whoever speaks against the Holy Spirit will not be forgiven
in this world or the next."
Matthew 12:31-32 (GW)

Who is The Holy Spirit?

(Jesus speaking)
"If you love me, you will obey my commandments.
I will ask the Father, and he will give you another helper
who will be with you forever.
That helper is the <u>Spirit of Truth</u>.
The world cannot accept him, because it doesn't see or know him.

You know him, because he lives with you and will be in you.
I will not leave you all alone. I will come back to you.
In a little while the world will no longer see me,
but you will see me.
You will live because I live.
On that day you will know that I am in my Father
and that you are in me and that I am in you."
John 14:15-20 (GW)

(Jesus speaking)
"When the Spirit of Truth comes,
he will guide you into the full truth.
He won't speak on his own.
He will speak what he hears
and will tell you about things to come."
John 16:13 (GW)

The Holy Spirit is The Spirit of Truth, Who testifies of God and Jesus. To believe The Truth is to experience freedom and joy unending. Refusing to believe The Truth and even worse, actively working against The Truth puts one in the camp of the "father of lies."

Jesus' Words apply to those who have come to know The Truth and have still rejected and worked against The Truth.

It is possible that people can commit evil acts, because they do not truly know God, Jesus and The Holy Spirit. Such was the case of those who crucified Jesus. They believed they were doing good when they were doing evil. Jesus had mercy on them and asked for forgiveness for them. Why? He said they didn't know what they were doing.

Then Jesus said, "Father, forgive them.
They don't know what they're doing. ..."
Luke 23:34 (GW)

Saul, the terrorist, thought he was persecuting Christians because he was serving God. Even though he thought he knew God, he did not. His acts were evil, but he did not know The Truth yet. However, when he did know The Truth, he completely changed.

If you receive The Truth revealed to you, repent of anything that would ever separate you from Him again and walk in the Way He directs, you have nothing to worry about. If you reject The Holy Spirit, who leads you into the Whole Truth, you have made a choice that puts you in clear opposition to God. Jesus contrasted who needs to be afraid and who does not need to be afraid.

(Jesus' Message to those who reject The Truth)
"My friends,
I can guarantee that you don't need to be afraid of those who kill the body.
After that they can't do anything more.
I'll show you the one you should be afraid of.
Be afraid of the one who has the power to throw you into hell
after killing you.
I'm warning you to be afraid of him."

(Jesus' Message to those who believe The Truth)
"Aren't five sparrows sold for two cents?
God doesn't forget any of them.
Even every hair on your head has been counted.
Don't be afraid! You are worth more than many sparrows."
Luke 12:4-7 (GW)

Chapter 6

What Goes Around, Comes Around!

O nce we have discovered the One inside us, we may wish to just wrap up in God's Love and float happily. It may be a shock to our system to discover that there are other people on this planet and God wants us to love them all.

Much of Jesus' Mission to save us from our sins had to do with our relationship with other people.

(Jesus speaking)
"I'm giving you a new commandment:
Love each other in the same way that I have loved you."
John 13:34 (GW)

Jesus answered him,
"'Love the Lord your God with all your heart,
with all your soul, and with all your mind.'
This is the greatest and most important commandment.
The second is like it:
'Love your neighbor as you love yourself.'
All of Moses' Teachings and the Prophets depend on these two
commandments."
Matthew 22:37-40 (GW)

Jesus was not giving a suggestion. He was giving a command! He made it clear we were to love one another, not just with limited human love, but with Love, as He loved us. To begin to understand how to love others, Jesus said we should start with what we knew. How would we like to be loved?

"Do for other people everything you want them to do for you."
Luke 6:31 (GW)

Besides giving us the "training wheels" of how to love, Jesus was also calling attention to an important principle of the Universe. What you send out returns to you and in large measure. If you send out good, good will return to you. If you send out evil, evil will return.

Jesus illustrated this principle in His Sermon on the Mount.

"Blessed are those who show mercy. They will be treated mercifully."
Matthew 5:7 (GW)

The ultimate example of Love is always The One—God, Jesus and The Holy Spirit.

Be kind to each other, sympathetic,
forgiving each other
as God has forgiven you through Christ.
Ephesians 4:32 (GW)

How did Jesus forgive? He forgave those who were loyal to Him and He forgave those some might classify as His enemies. He asked His Father to forgive those who were crucifying Him. He told us to forgive our enemies.

"But I tell you this: Love your enemies,
and pray for those who persecute you."
Matthew 5:44 (GW)

"Wait!" you might say. "That's a pretty tall order. You don't know what these people have done to me." If you are hesitant to forgive, be sure to understand that you are on the verge of committing a sin for which you will not be forgiven.

(Jesus speaking)
"For if you forgive other people when they sin against you,
your heavenly Father will also forgive you.
But if you do not forgive others their sins,
your Father will not forgive your sins."
Matthew 6:14-15 (NIV2011)

Our lack of forgiveness means God cannot forgive us. The good news is that when we repent and forgive, God will forgive us.

When we decide who deserves our forgiveness, we are setting ourselves up as judge and jury. Jesus was also very plain spoken about the dangers of judging others.

"Stop judging so that you will not be judged.
Otherwise, you will be judged by the same standard you use to judge others.
The standards you use for others will be applied to you."
Matthew 7:1-2 (GW)

As recorded in The Gospel of Matthew, Chapter 18, Verses 23 through 35, Jesus told the parable of one who was forgiven much, but refused to forgive others. Jesus' story ends detailing the anger of the master who had forgiven the one who refused to forgive. In a chilling climax to Jesus' story, He said,

"His master was so angry
that he handed him over to the torturers
until he would repay everything that he owed.
That is what my Father in heaven will do to you
if each of you does not sincerely forgive other believers."
Matthew 18:34-35 (GW)

Jesus continued to teach over and over again that we must forgive all.

> *"And when you stand praying,*
> *if you hold anything against anyone, forgive them,*
> *so that your Father in heaven may forgive you your sins."*
> *Mark 11:25 (NIV2011)*

When His Disciples asked Jesus how to pray, He taught them what we now call The Lord's Prayer. Many of us can recite it from memory. Memorizing scripture is always a great way to plant The Word of God in our hearts and minds. However, the danger of familiarity is that we can then recite it without thinking about it.

Read The Gospel of Matthew, Chapter 6, Verses 9 through 13. Carefully think about every word. Jesus specifically addressed the need to forgive.

> *"Forgive us as we forgive others."*
> *Matthew 6:12 (GW)*

We often miss what Jesus said right after He shared The Lord's Prayer. To emphasize the importance of forgiving others, Jesus added:

> *"For if you forgive other people when they sin against you,*
> *your heavenly Father will also forgive you.*
> *But if you do not forgive others their sins,*
> *your Father will not forgive your sins."*
> *Matthew 6:14-15 (NIV2011)*

Sometimes we fail to tell others the Whole Truth when we "lead them to Christ." We correctly tell them to repent of their sins and receive God's Forgiveness. But we neglect to tell them God's Forgiveness has some conditions. We forget to tell them there is a specific need to forgive others as well as asking God's Forgiveness for themselves.

Chapter 7

Gone, But Not Forgotten

*S*in that is in any way attached to us will separate us from seeing, hearing and feeling God's Presence. It will keep us from receiving all God wants to give us.

Refusing to forgive is responsible for the seeds of bitterness and distrust that satan would like to sow within us. When we think of the wrongs that were committed against us or others, we are often angry. Something in us demands our brand of justice. We may not be able to satisfy the desire to retaliate. So, often we imprison the offenders within the jails of our minds.

It takes effort to constantly check on the prisoners. In fact, it is we who are in prison. Often the ones who are the object of our anger do not even realize how we feel about them.

Constantly reviewing what happened to us also creates an ongoing distrust of others. We may see everyone as having the potential to hurt us. We are not so likely to enter relationships we cannot control.

Satan attempts to plant seeds that grow into roots of bitterness, reaching far into our mind. He wants us to distrust God. He wants us to believe God did not care enough about us to bring about our brand of justice. He wants us to believe we have to deal with those who sin against us. He tempts us to withhold forgiveness. And he has a variety of ways to entice us to further sin in our anger.

Do not let anger grow into the bitter root.

> *Make sure that everyone has kindness from God*
> *so that bitterness doesn't take root*
> *and grow up to cause trouble that corrupts many of you.*
> *Hebrews 12:15 (GW)*

> *"In your anger do not sin":*
> *Do not let the sun go down while you are still angry,*
> *and do not give the devil a foothold.*
> *Ephesians 4:26-27 (NIV2011)*

Once we understand The Truth that if we do not forgive, God will not forgive us, we may be in distress because we do not know how to forgive.

We try to forgive and forget, but it does not work. Unlike God, Who does not remember confessed and repented sin any more, we remember. Often we try to put the person who committed the sin out of our mind completely. But this is especially difficult if they are still in our present life. It is not God's intent that we attempt to "sweep them under the rug."

It is God's Desire that we recognize our Oneness in Him. It is His Desire that we see each other as He sees us. We are all created in His Image, but we are all prone to sin and in need of God's Forgiveness.

When we want to begin again in writing, using our computer, we hit "delete" and we type a new line. If we type the same word, it will be back in front of us again. If we type something different, the old will be gone and the new will appear.

If you want to begin again, simply ask God to reveal to you anyone you have not forgiven. Then ask Him to show you how to forgive. After you have repented of the sin of unforgiveness, you will be better able to see and hear God.

Agree with God and delete the sins of the one who acted against you. Pray for them, using God's Words to describe people at their best. Believe God is working out His Plan for that person, so others will see Him in them. Trust Him to do what He has promised to do.

God always agrees with us, when we agree with what He has said in His Word. Pray, seeing the person as a new creature in Christ Jesus.

Believe The Spirit of Truth that assures us The Light will outshine the darkness. Good will triumph over evil. Believe The Word of God is active and that what He says will apply to anyone He created.

Confess God's Love right now, as recorded in 1st Corinthians. Read through this scripture three times. The first time, read it as it is written. The second time, insert God's Name of "I AM," as I will illustrate to you. The third time, insert the name of the one you have had difficulty forgiving, and believe in faith that God will verify the Truth of His Love.

Love is patient, love is kind.
It does not envy, it does not boast, it is not proud.
It does not dishonor others,
it is not self-seeking,
it is not easily angered,
it keeps no record of wrongs.
Love does not delight in evil but rejoices with the truth.
It always protects, always trusts, always hopes,
always perseveres.

Love never fails. …
1 Corinthians 13:4-8 (NIV2011)

I AM patient, I AM kind.
I do not envy, I do not boast, I AM not proud.
I do not dishonor others,
I AM not self-seeking,
I AM not easily angered,
I keep no record of wrongs.
I do not delight in evil, but I rejoice in the truth.
I will always protect, always trust, always hope,
always persevere.

God's Love in me never fails.

(Insert the name of the one you forgive. We will use the name, John, as an
example here.)

John is patient, John is kind.
John does not envy, John does not boast, John is not proud.
John does not dishonor others,
John is not self-seeking,
John is not easily angered,
John keeps no record of wrongs.
John does not delight in evil, but John rejoices in the truth.
John always protects, always trusts, always hopes,
always perseveres.
God's Love in John never fails.

Chapter 8

Why Won't God Weed His Garden?

*A*fter we have recognized The One within us, we have forgiven others and we have repented of our sins, we may be feeling pretty good. We believe ourselves ready to live life with Jesus and go where He wants to go. We look forward to hanging out with other people who love Him as much as we do.

But it turns out He is not going there. He wants to spend the day with people who don't know Him and some don't even seem like they are interested in knowing Him. Some are clearly on the side of evil. So what is up with that?

Even our friends may be baffled as to why we are hanging out with the old crowd. Weren't we supposed to avoid evil? Yes, we are to avoid evil itself. With our new life, hopefully we will be better able to detect evil and be sure we are wearing The Whole Armor of God. But we will be a part of Jesus' Rescue Team, going to help fulfill His Mission.

…Jesus said to them,
"It is not the healthy who need a doctor, but the sick.
I have not come to call the righteous, but sinners."
Mark 2:17 (NIV2011)

What if we call the sinners and they still stay sinners? Shouldn't we eliminate them, so they don't spoil things for the rest of us … you know, the righteous ones like us?

When we reach a point where we cannot see our kinship with the unrighteous, we are in trouble. While we want to recognize our kinship with Jesus, we have already looked at how hard it is to maintain God's Standard of Perfection. We are not righteous in ourselves. The ones we brand as evil are not righteous either.

When Jesus' Disciples asked Him about what should be done with those who are not following Him, He told a most interesting parable.

> … *"The kingdom of heaven is like a man*
> *who planted good seed in his field.*
> *But while people were asleep,*
> *his enemy planted weeds in the wheat field and went away.*
> *When the wheat came up and formed kernels, weeds appeared.*
>
> *"The owner's workers came to him and asked,*
> *'Sir, didn't you plant good seed in your field?*
> *Where did the weeds come from?'*
>
> *"He told them, 'An enemy did this.'*
>
> *"His workers asked him, 'Do you want us to pull out the weeds?'*
> *"He replied, 'No. If you pull out the weeds,*
> *you may pull out the wheat with them.*
> *Let both grow together until the harvest.*
> *When the grain is cut, I will tell the workers*
> *to gather the weeds first and tie them in bundles*
> *to be burned.*
> *But I'll have them bring the wheat into my barn.'"*
> *Matthew 13:24-30 (GW)*

199

The Kingdom on earth in which we now live has a variety of things growing. We are all in a state of becoming what God created us to be. It is to the benefit of all for all to recognize The Master Gardener is in charge. He alone decides when and how to tend His Garden.

Our forgiveness of others should extend beyond people we know. We watch the evening news and see the victims of evil. We pray for them. But less often do we see the ones committing the evil acts as victims of satan. Less often do we follow Jesus' lead and forgive them, praying for them to come to know The One.

When we forgive, we should forgive those who do not yet know they are sinning. If we are to participate in the ongoing Mission of Jesus, we must remember The Word of The Lord, Who said,

> ... *"I don't want wicked people to die.*
> *Rather, I want them to turn from their ways and live."* ...
> *Ezekiel 33:11 (GW)*

Peter reminded us also,

> *The Lord isn't slow to do what he promised,*
> *as some people think.*
> *Rather, he is patient for your sake.*
> *He doesn't want to destroy anyone*
> *but wants all people to have an opportunity to turn to him*
> *and change the way they think and act.*
> *2 Peter 3:9 (GW)*

What if God had weeded His Garden before we knew Him? Praise God, He was patient with us. May we extend His Grace and Mercy to others!

Chapter 9

Grace

We may be puzzled about whether Jesus gave some people a free pass to forgiveness. It seems some did not have to repent or forgive others before they were forgiven.

They took baby steps toward Jesus, expecting He was Who He said He was and could do what He said He could do. They put themselves in a position of humility and were ready to receive what Jesus had for them. They believed! There are many examples of the miracles that happened when humility and belief connected with Jesus' Power and Authority.

In the story of the paralyzed man, Jesus made it clear He had both Power and Authority to forgive sins and to heal sicknesses.

Some people brought him a paralyzed man on a stretcher.
When Jesus saw their faith, he said to the man,
"Cheer up, friend! Your sins are forgiven."

Then some of the scribes thought,
"He's dishonoring God."

Jesus knew what they were thinking. He asked them,
"Why are you thinking evil things?
Is it easier to say, 'Your sins are forgiven,'
or to say, 'Get up and walk'?
I want you to know that the Son of Man
has authority on earth to forgive sins."
Then he said to the paralyzed man,
"Get up, pick up your stretcher, and go home."
Matthew 9:2-6 (GW)

Another example recorded is the day Jesus connected with two men who were blind.

When Jesus left that place,
two blind men followed him. They shouted,
"Have mercy on us, Son of David."

Jesus went into a house, and the blind men followed him.
He said to them,
"Do you believe that I can do this?"
"Yes, Lord," they answered.

He touched their eyes and said,
"What you have believed will be done for you!"
Then they could see. ...
Matthew 9:27-30 (GW)

When Jesus saw the humility and the desire of the sick to be healed, He was moved with Compassion. When He saw they believed He had all Power and Authority to heal them, He credited it to them as righteousness.

Humble yourselves before the Lord, and he will lift you up.
James 4:10 (NIV2011)

Abram believed the LORD,
and he credited it to him as righteousness.
Genesis 15:6 (NIV2011)

Jesus first gave them the Gift of forgiving their sins. With their sins gone, the obstacles to receiving healing were gone. The line between Jesus, The Healer and the ones soon to be healed was clear. Every cell in their body heard The Call to obey The One, and they did so.

"…I am the Lord, who heals you."
Exodus 15:26 (NIV2011)

Chapter 10

Will God Take His Gifts Back?

*D*id those who were healed get to keep the Gifts they received? When God gives us Gifts, will He ever take them back? He does not want to take them back.

> *God never changes his mind when he gives gifts*
> *or when he calls someone.*
> *Romans 11:29 (GW)*

However, there are at least two examples that illustrate the possibility that God might take back Gifts that are used wrongly or not used at all.

There was an example given by Jesus of the displeasure of the master, who had given gifts of money to three different men. The first two men used their money and through wise investments, grew it. The master was pleased.

However, the third man buried his money and did nothing with it. The master did take his money away. Why? It was not because he made a foolish business decision, but because of the attitude that demonstrated clearly he did not know the master. He did not trust him. He thought negative things about him.

He was afraid of him. He had chosen in his heart to keep what the master had given him, but not to have a relationship with him.

> *"Then the one who received two thousand dollars came and said,*
> *'Sir, I knew that you are a hard person to please.*
> *You harvest where you haven't planted*
> *and gather where you haven't scattered any seeds.*
> *I was afraid. So I hid your two thousand dollars in the ground.*
> *Here's your money!'*
>
> *"His master responded,*
> *'You evil and lazy servant!*
> *If you knew that I harvest where I haven't planted*
> *and gather where I haven't scattered,*
> *then you should have invested my money with the bankers.*
> *When I returned, I would have received my money back with interest.*
> *Take the two thousand dollars away from him!*
> *Give it to the one who has the ten thousand!*
> *To all who have, more will be given,*
> *and they will have more than enough.*
> *But everything will be taken away from those who don't have much.*
> *Throw this useless servant outside into the darkness.*
> *People will cry and be in extreme pain there.'"*
> *Matthew 25:24-30 (GW)*

We need to carefully inventory all the Lord has given us, and consider whether we are using His Gifts to bring Glory to Him. Paul wisely spoke when he said,

> *…whatever you do, do everything to the glory of God.*
> *1 Corinthians 10:31 (GW)*

When Jesus was speaking to the Church at Ephesus, He said:

"However, I have this against you:
The love you had at first is gone.
Remember how far you have fallen.
Return to me and change the way you think and act,
and do what you did at first.
I will come to you
and take your lamp stand from its place if you don't change."
Revelation 2:4-5 (GW)

Jesus was concerned the church had forsaken the love they had at first for Him. They had fallen far. If they did not repent, He would take His Gift back.

This brings up the important question of whether once we are saved, are we always saved? Let's look closer at what being "saved" means.

Chapter 11

Saved and Being Saved!

*J*esus' Mission on earth was to save us from sin and the wages of sin, which would be paid us by satan. His Mission was to assure that we had eternal life, not eternal death.

> " ... *you are to give him the name Jesus,*
> *because he will save his people from their sins."*
> *Matthew 1:21 (NIV2011)*

> *For the wages of sin is death,*
> *but the gift of God is eternal life in Christ Jesus our Lord.*
> *Romans 6:23 (NIV2011)*

> *(Jesus speaking)*
> *"This is eternal life: to know you, the only true God,*
> *and Jesus Christ, whom you sent."*
> *John 17:3 (GW)*

It is a misnomer to say that on a given day, we "invited Jesus in" and it was a "one and done" event. It is more accurate to say that at a given time, we discovered The One Who had been in us from the beginning, and that every moment since that time, we have celebrated His Presence within us.

Being saved from sin is an ongoing process. Just as we need food, water and oxygen to keep our physical body functioning, we need regular nourishment from The Bread of Life, Living Water and The Breath of The Holy Spirit to keep our spiritual body functioning.

The physical body has various ways to cast off the waste products of our body. These functions are carried out *regularly*. In our spiritual life, we must *regularly* seek to know what we are to cast off. We need to *regularly* repent and be freed of our sins. We need to *regularly* forgive others and be freed of the sins that try to attach themselves to us through unforgiveness.

Timothy, Paul and Peter all referred to the *ongoing and present process* of being saved. For them, it was not a singular event of the past. It was an ongoing Gift to be celebrated constantly.

He has saved us and called us to a <u>holy life</u>—
not because of anything we have done
but because of his own purpose and grace.
This grace was given us in Christ Jesus before the beginning of time,
2 Timothy 1:9 (NIV2011)

For the message of the cross is foolishness
to those who are perishing,
but to us who are <u>being saved</u> it is the power of God.
1 Corinthians 1:18 (NIV2011)

Though you have not seen him, you love him;
and even though you do not see him now, you believe in him
and are filled with an inexpressible and glorious joy,
for <u>you are receiving</u> the end result of your faith,
the salvation of your souls.
1 Peter 1:8-9 (NIV2011)
(Underline added for emphasis)

Jesus underscored the Gift of the process of ongoing salvation. Many become accustomed to communion as a periodic event. However, this is not what Jesus intended. He wanted us to remember what He had done for us and to realize The Truth of His Imparting Statement of His Ongoing Presence. He keyed our remembering to something we would be doing multiple times in a day.

Jesus said to remember His Covenant with us *each* time we eat and drink. We would experience the Joy of our Salvation if we took Him at His Word, and stopped and really praised and thanked Him before we ate or drank anything. I challenge you to remember The One *every* time you eat or drink.

> *When supper was over, he did the same with the cup.*
> *He said, "This cup is the new promise made with my blood.*
> *Every time you drink from it, do it to remember me."*
> *Every time you eat this bread and drink from this cup,*
> *you tell about the Lord's death until he comes.*
> *1 Corinthians 11:25-26 (GW)*

Chapter 12

Can We Lose Our Salvation?

*C*an we lose this marvelous Gift of Salvation? We can choose to go another way and leave Fellowship with The One. We can throw His Gift away. We can believe we are pushing Him far away. We can deny His Presence, but it will not change the reality that He still lives within us.

As regularly as our heart beats and our lungs bring in fresh air, He will call to us from within. He will seek us out wherever we go. We belong to Him, not because we chose Him, but because He chose us. We are together eternally.

"You did not choose me, but I chose you
and appointed you so that you might go and bear fruit—
fruit that will last—
and so that whatever you ask in my name the Father will give you."
John 15:16 (NIV2011)

Where can I go from your Spirit?
Where can I flee from your presence?
If I go up to the heavens, you are there;
if I make my bed in the depths, you are there.
If I rise on the wings of the dawn,

If I settle on the far side of the sea,
even there your hand will guide me,
your right hand will hold me fast.
Psalm 139:7-10 (NIV2011)

(Jesus speaking)
"What do you think?
Suppose a man has 100 sheep and one of them strays.
Won't he leave the 99 sheep in the hills
to look for the one that has strayed?
I can guarantee this truth: If he finds it,
he is happier about it
than about the 99 that have not strayed.
In the same way, your Father in heaven
does not want one of these little ones to be lost."
Matthew 18:12-14 (GW)

But now comes a significant Word of Caution. Jesus expected fruit from the seeds He planted within us.

"…I chose you and appointed you
so that you might go and bear fruit—fruit that will last—
and so that whatever you ask in my name the Father will give you."
John 15:16 (NIV2011)

How do we bear fruit? By staying attached to the vine. Who is our Spiritual Vine? Jesus. Who are we? The Branches. Who is The Gardener? God.

God gives us everything we need to enjoy Life in this world and to produce More Life for the world. However, He does not tolerate dead branches. When what was created as Life becomes dead, God will remove it. The following Words are both a comfort and a warning.

(Jesus speaking)
"I am the true vine, and my Father is the gardener.
He cuts off every branch in me that bears no fruit,
while every branch that does bear fruit he prunes
so that it will be even more fruitful.
You are already clean because of the word I have spoken to you.
Remain in me, as I also remain in you.
No branch will can bear fruit by itself; it must remain in the vine.
Neither can you bear fruit unless you remain in me.

"I am the vine; you are the branches.
If you remain in me and I in you, you will bear much fruit;
apart from me you can do nothing.
If you do not remain in me,
you are like a branch that is thrown away and withers;
such branches are picked up, thrown into the fire and burned.
If you remain in me and my words remain in you,
ask whatever you wish, and it will be done for you.
This is to my Father's glory, that you bear much fruit,
showing yourselves to be my disciples."
John 15:1-8 (NIV2011)

Chapter 13

Truth or Fiction?

We have explored The Truth that "salvation" is an ongoing process as opposed to a one-time event. However, we cannot deny that one very significant event—the crucifixion of Jesus Christ—is at the center of many of our Christian beliefs about salvation.

Many misconceptions have crept into what we have come to call The Easter Story. Let's look at the way the story is often told, and determine whether what we have heard is consistent with what we know about God and His Love for us.

You Can't Separate The One!

God and Jesus are often presented as separate. God, Jesus and The Holy Spirit have been together from the beginning, are and ever shall be. Jesus' other name of Immanuel verifies Jesus is "God with us." Jesus repeatedly told us that He is in The Father and The Father is in Him.

(Jesus speaking)
"Believe me when I say that I am in the Father
and that the Father is in me. ..."
John 14:11 (GW)

213

"The Father and I are one."
John 10:30 (GW)

God, Jesus and The Holy Spirit were all together during every second of Jesus' torture and crucifixion.

Is God Abusive, Vengeful and Angry with Us?

Satan would have us believe that God is a very abusive, vengeful God, Who would really like to beat us senseless for committing sins. Then He would like to kill us in a very public ugly death. He would do this so that everyone would remember and be warned they could be the next one to be punished in such a way by God. But does what satan says line up with what we know about God?

(God speaking)
"I love you with an everlasting love.
So I will continue to show you my kindness."
Jeremiah 31:3 (GW)

The LORD is merciful, compassionate,
patient, and always ready to forgive.
The LORD is good to everyone
and has compassion for everything that he has made.
Psalm 145:8-9 (GW)

(Jesus speaking)
"Be merciful as your Father is merciful."
Luke 6:36 (GW)

Does God Approve of Human Sacrifice?

God is sometimes presented as being in favor of human sacrifice. Nothing could be further from The Truth. There are scriptures that speak to God's condemnation of the pagans who sacrificed their children to idols.

When you enter the land the LORD your God is giving you,
do not learn to imitate the detestable ways of the nations there.
Let no one be found among you
who sacrifices their son or daughter in the fire,
who practices divination or sorcery, interprets omens,
engages in witchcraft, or casts spells,
or who is a medium or spiritist or who consults the dead.
Anyone who does these things is detestable to the LORD; ...
Deuteronomy 18:9-12 (NIV2011)

Wait! Didn't God tell Abraham to sacrifice his son, Isaac? Why would God do that if He didn't approve of human sacrifice?

God had promised Abraham that his seed would be more numerous than the stars in the sky. God had told him specifically that these blessings would come through Isaac. Then it appeared that God was telling Abraham to sacrifice Isaac. Could this be what God wanted?

No. God wanted Abraham to put Him in remembrance of His Word. He wanted Abraham to think of Who God was and what He would say and do. God did not want Abraham (or us) to get taken in by believing God was telling us to do something that was far removed from His Nature. God was both testing and teaching Abraham.

Sometimes when we are trying to teach children, we say to them, "What did I say?" Is it that we do not remember? No. We remember, but we want them to tell us, so they remember.

The classic line many parents have said to their teenagers, who are bowing to peer pressure, is, "If I tell you to go jump off a bridge, are you going to do it?" Would we ever ask such a thing of them? No! We are teaching them to remember what we have taught them and not be swayed by anything different.

What God desired from Abraham was a "push back." He wanted him to say, "But God, you promised me that my seed would be as numerous as the stars in the sky. Besides that, you find human sacrifice detestable. The pagans do that. We don't do that."

Many misunderstand the story of Abraham and Isaac to mean that God directed Abraham to sacrifice Isaac to prove his love and obedience to God. However, this is not what God had in mind. He wanted Abraham to know Him and to know beyond a shadow of a doubt that He would not demand human sacrifice. Neither would God go back on what He promised Abraham He would give him through Isaac. This was a test from God, not an endorsement of human sacrifice.

... God tested Abraham ...
Genesis 22:1 (GW)

If God Is Really Just, Wouldn't He Have to Punish Sinners?
Many understand that God is just. They know He cannot approve sin. So therefore, they believe it He would want to condemn and punish severely those who sin. Satan would like us to believe that when we sin, we become wicked and God wants to eliminate all wicked people. Satan does not mention to us that God has allowed him to continue living. Let's see what God says about eliminating the wicked.

"Tell them,
'As I live, declares the Almighty LORD,
I don't want wicked people to die.
Rather, I want them to turn from their ways and live. ...'"
Ezekiel 33:11 (GW)

... Rather, he is patient for your sake. He doesn't want to destroy anyone
but wants all people to have an opportunity
to turn to him and change the way they think and act.
2 Peter 3:9 (GW)

God is faithful and reliable. If we confess our sins,
he forgives them
and cleanses us from everything we've done wrong.
1 John 1:9 (GW)

God sent his Son into the world, not to condemn the world,
but to save the world.
John 3:17 (GW)

How Could God Be Both Just and Loving?

Some believe that if God is just, then it follows He would have to judge, sentence and carry out the sentence for sin. So, they reason, since God is loving, He didn't give everyone what they deserved. He let Jesus take their place. They look for other places where it appeared God wanted evil people to die and conclude it must be ok to kill a human, if it is for a good reason.

God set a very high standard on how He views the taking of life that He created. God holds Himself to the same standard He holds us. This is what He says about killing one He created.

"You shall not murder."
Exodus 20:13 (NIV2011)

(Killing an innocent man would certainly be murder.)
And for your lifeblood I will surely demand an accounting.
I will demand an accounting from every animal.
And from each human being, too,
I will demand an accounting for the life of another human being."
Genesis 9:5 (NIV2011)

God was not giving permission for humans to shed blood in revenge for blood being shed. He was simply making a statement that shedding one person's blood will inevitably lead to more shedding of blood.

When Peter impulsively cut off the ear of the High Priest's servant, Jesus repeated the lesson that violence toward another human would only lead to more violence.

Suddenly, one of the men with Jesus pulled out his sword
and cut off the ear of the chief priest's servant.

Then Jesus said to him,
"Put your sword away!
All who use a sword will be killed by a sword."
Matthew 26:51-52 (GW)

Because we are humans made in the Image of God, He values us highly and does not approve anyone killing us. God would never approve killing a Part of Himself.

If God Did Not Make Jesus Die As a Human Sacrifice, What Happened?

Here we get to the most amazing Truth of all. If God wasn't separate from Jesus and He didn't order a hit on His Own Son ... and if He does not approve of human sacrifice or murdering an innocent man ... then what was the cross all about? The crux of the matter is in Jesus' Statement ...

"No one takes my life [Jesus' Life] from me.
I give my life of my own free will.
I have the authority to give my life,
and I have the authority to take my life back again.
This is what my Father ordered me to do."
John 10:18 (GW)

And when Jesus had cried out again in a loud voice,
he gave up his spirit.
Matthew 27:50 (NIV2011)

218

Jesus was not a victim. God, Jesus and The Holy Spirit had a Plan to rescue their people from their sins. All three parts of The One were together at the cross, as the Victory Team. Together They chose the ultimate way to define Good and Evil and to rescue Their Creations from death.

Let's move forward and see how They carried out Their Amazing Plan! To understand The Plan, you will need to familiarize yourself with a Celebration very familiar to the Jews. Passover was a wonderful event to be remembered, but the actual event was in the past.

However, there was another event that happened regularly in the future. It was called the Year of The Lord's Favor or Jubilee.

Chapter 14

The Year of Jubilee

*T*he Lord taught His People a unique way of blessing each other every seven years.

> *At the end of every seven years you must cancel debts.*
> *This is how it is to be done:*
> *Every creditor shall cancel any loan*
> *they have made to a fellow Israelite.*
> *They shall not require payment from anyone among their own people,*
> *because the LORD's time for canceling debts has been proclaimed.*
> *Deuteronomy 15:1-2 (NIV2011)*

It gets even better.

> *If any of your people—Hebrew men or women—*
> *sell themselves to you and serve you six years,*
> *in the seventh year you must let them go free.*
> *And when you release them, do not send them away empty-handed.*
> *Supply them liberally from your flock,*
> *your threshing floor and your winepress.*
> *Give to them as the LORD your God has blessed you.*
> *Deuteronomy 15:12-14 (NIV2011)*

What a wonderful gift to have all your debts cancelled and to be freed of slavery with blessings of provision as you go.

But in the fiftieth year, there was a mega-celebration. It was called the Jubilee (also called The Year of The Lord's Favor).

All land on which the Israelites lived was correctly recognized as belonging to God. They, as are we, are tenants living on God's Property here on earth.

After seven sets of seven years were completed, the next year—the fiftieth year—was designated as the year of Jubilee. Each Jubilee Year marked a time of celebration when everyone received back their original property and slaves returned home in freedom to their families.

> *"'Count off seven sabbath years—seven times seven years—*
> *so that the seven sabbath years amount to a period of*
> *forty-nine years.*
> *Then have the trumpet sounded everywhere*
> *on the tenth day of the seventh month;*
> *on the Day of Atonement sound the trumpet throughout your land.*
> *Consecrate the fiftieth year and*
> *proclaim liberty throughout the land to all its inhabitants.*
> *It shall be a jubilee for you;*
> *each of you is to return to your family property and to your own clan.*
> *The fiftieth year shall be a jubilee for you;*
> *do not sow and do not reap what grows of itself*
> *or harvest the untended vines.*
> *For it is a jubilee and is to be holy for you;*
> *eat only what is taken directly from the fields.*
> *"'In this Year of Jubilee everyone is to return to their own property.'"*
> *Leviticus 25:8-13 (NIV2011)*

It was a grand Homecoming, but not nearly as grand as the Homecoming God was planning to reveal through Jesus.

Now let's fast forward to Jesus' time. Let's join Him at The Temple. Listen carefully. Something extraordinary is about to happen!

Chapter 15

A Fantastic Preview of A Jubilee Like No Other!

(Scripture refers to Jesus)
He went to Nazareth, where he had been brought up,
and on the Sabbath day he went into the synagogue,
as was his custom.

He stood up to read,
and the scroll of the prophet Isaiah was handed to him.
Unrolling it, he found the place where it is written:

"The Spirit of the Lord is on me,
because he has anointed me
to proclaim good news to the poor.
He has sent me to proclaim freedom for the prisoners
and recovery of sight for the blind,
to set the oppressed free,
to proclaim the year of the Lord's favor."

Then he rolled up the scroll,
gave it back to the attendant and sat down.
The eyes of everyone in the synagogue were fastened on him.
He began by saying to them,
"Today this scripture is fulfilled in your hearing."
Luke 4:16-21 (NIV2011)

Jesus was there to do all that the Jubilee Year was intended to do. He was there to set free those who had been oppressed, as a slave to satan. He was there to give all people a new way of looking at God and the world around them. He was there to restore the spiritual riches they had been given from the beginning of the world. He was there to point them Home.

Interestingly, Jesus stopped before reading the rest of the Prophet Isaiah, Chapter 61, Verse 2, which included, "and the day of vengeance of our God." There was no vengeance from God through Jesus. There was only Love and Mercy.

Isaiah also saw the beauty that was about to be revealed through Jesus. He saw a crown, but not of thorns. He saw oil, but not oil of covering the stench of death. He saw a garment, not one taken off of a dying man, but one that covered His Living Relatives.

> *... to comfort all who mourn,*
> *and provide for those who grieve in Zion—*
> *to bestow on them a crown of beauty instead of ashes,*
> *the oil of joy instead of mourning,*
> *and a garment of praise instead of a spirit of despair.*
> *They will be called oaks of righteousness,*
> *a planting of the LORD for the display of his splendor.*
> *Isaiah 61:2-3 (NIV2011)*

Chapter 16

God's Memorable Lesson

*B*efore the splendor, we need to look straight on at the message of the cross. We now know that God, Jesus and The Holy Spirit are one and they were all there at the cross. We know that they came to rescue those held by satan. How did they accomplish this by making the people see horrible images of torture and death?

Jesus gave us a clue that is rarely, if ever, referenced in the Easter story. And yet, it is highly significant in explaining the cross.

(Jesus speaking)
"Just as Moses lifted up the snake in the wilderness,
so the Son of Man must be lifted up,
that everyone who believes may have eternal life in him."
John 3:14-15 (NIV2011)

In order to understand what Jesus is talking about, we must go back to Moses.

Then they moved from Mount Hor, following the road that goes to
the Red Sea,
in order to get around Edom.

The people became impatient on the trip
and criticized God and Moses. They said,
"Why did you make us leave Egypt—just to let us die in the desert?
There's no bread or water,
and we can't stand this awful food!"

So the LORD sent poisonous snakes among the people.
They bit the people, and many of the Israelites died.
The people came to Moses and said,
"We sinned when we criticized the LORD and you.
Pray to the LORD so that he will take the snakes away from us."
So Moses prayed for the people.

The LORD said to Moses,
"Make a snake, and put it on a pole.
Anyone who is bitten can look at it and live."
So Moses made a bronze snake and put it on a pole.
People looked at the bronze snake after they were bitten,
and they lived.
Numbers 21:4-9 (GW)

Why would God do such a thing? Wasn't he opposed to idols? Didn't He say not to make any graven images? Why did He want the people to look at the symbol of satan? Most puzzling of all, why would staring at a bronze snake bring about their healing?

Let's go back to the beginning … all the way back to Adam and Eve. When they chose to open the door to the knowledge of good and evil, satan was able to put his foot in the door. He was able to blur the lines between what was good and what was evil.

It appeared that humans then, as now, vacillated back and forth between good and evil. All too often we end up with one foot on the side of evil and one foot on the side of good, not sure which way to go.

God wanted his people to know the distinct difference between good and evil. He wanted them to know that choosing good would result in blessings. Choosing evil would result in curses.

The people sinned in speaking against God and Moses. God allowed venomous snakes to bite them. The people had heard the stories from their youth of Adam and Eve and the serpent. They knew snakes were equated with evil. God was teaching them the consequences of choosing evil.

What God wanted was for His People to trust Him and obey Him in whatever He told them to do. He wanted them to recognize how He had provided for them and to be thankful. The people were humbled by their helplessness to combat the snakes. They repented.

God had Moses put the bronze snake on the pole, not to be worshipped, but to emblazon on their memory what evil looked like. He also wanted them to realize that evil had no power to heal them. It only had the power they had given it to hurt them.

It was obedience to God that brought their healing.

So, in a time many years later, The One essentially told satan, "Take your best shot. Bring all the evil you've got and pile it on. Let's get it out in the open once and for all."

Satan must have been ecstatic. The thought of being able to have free reign at parading his wares in front of an audience was exhilarating! To have the opportunity to attack God Himself was an opportunity he had lived for, ever since his failed rebellion.

He must have prepared for the day, savoring and anticipating every detail. When the day came and he saw Jesus hanging on his cross of torture, satan believed that as soon as Jesus was cut down, he, satan, would rise in all power to rule the earth.

But something went terribly wrong in his plans. Jesus arose and satan was still on the ground. Even worse, satan's prisoners were gone! The world saw all of satan's evil exposed, and they didn't want it.

God exposed evil and offered a clear choice between Good and Evil.

This day I call the heavens and the earth as witnesses against you
that I have set before you life and death,
blessings and curses.
Now choose life,
so that you and your children may live.
Deuteronomy 30:19 (NIV2011)

The Way
of
The Cross
Leads Home!

Jesus said …
"The thief comes only to steal and kill and destroy;
I have come that they may have life,
and have it to the full."
John 10:10 (NIV2011)

As the time approached for him
to be taken up to heaven,
Jesus resolutely set out for Jerusalem.
Luke 9:51 (NIV2011)

Chapter 1

The Anointing

*J*ust a couple of days before Passover, Jesus was visiting a friend.

*... a woman came with an alabaster jar of very expensive perfume,
made of pure nard.
She broke the jar and poured the perfume on his head.*
Mark 14:3 (NIV2011)

Some of those present were indignant at what they saw as a waste. One even noted that it was worth a year's wages and could have been sold to benefit the poor.

Jesus told them to leave her alone.

*"... she has done a beautiful thing to me. ... She did what she could.
She poured perfume on my body beforehand to prepare for my burial.
Truly I tell you, whenever the gospel is preached throughout the world,
what she has done will also be told, in memory of her."*
Mark 14:6, 8-9 (NIV2011)

Satan was already losing. It is likely that the aroma of the nard was still on Jesus' skin right through the crucifixion. Its fragrance would linger in the nostrils of those who were nearby for a long time after that day.

For we are to God the pleasing aroma of Christ
among those who are being saved and those who are perishing.
To the one we are an aroma that brings death;
to the other, an aroma that brings life. ...
2 Corinthians 2:15-16 (NIV2011)

Chapter 2

Eat Me!

*J*esus shared a meal with His Disciples shortly before His Death. He never specifically called it The Last Supper. However, it was the last evening meal Jesus ate as a human on earth. At that supper, He fed the disciples bread and wine. However, when He broke the bread, He said something that was unlike any of the other times they had eaten together.

> *Then Jesus took bread and spoke a prayer of thanksgiving.*
> *He broke the bread, gave it to them, and said,*
> *"This is my body, which is given up for you.*
> *Do this to remember me."*
> *Luke 22:19 (GW)*

Some immediately link Jesus' Words to His Crucifixion, thinking of His Physical Body being broken. This line of thought seems to have come from the King James translation of Paul's Words.

> *and when He had given thanks, He brake it, and said,*
> *Take, eat: this is my body, which is broken for you:*
> *this do in remembrance of me.*
> *1 Corinthians 11:24 (KJV)*

However, God assured that the Bible verified in both the Old Testament and the New Testament that Jesus' Physical Body was never broken.

The LORD guards all of his bones.
Not one of them is broken.
Psalm 34:20 (GW)

The soldiers broke the legs of the first man
and then of the other man who had been crucified with Jesus.
When the soldiers came to Jesus
and saw that he was already dead,
they didn't break his legs.
John 19:32-33 (GW)

This happened so that the Scripture would come true:
"None of his bones will be broken."
John 19:36 (GW)

If Jesus was not talking about His physical Body being broken, then what was broken? Sometimes we look for symbolism, when what is being said is quite literal. However, literal can have symbolism too.

Jesus was calling attention to something He had done regularly with His Disciples and others. He had broken bread with them. He had fed His Followers both physical and spiritual bread. He had taught them how to feed others God's Word, the True Bread of Life.

God was speaking through Jesus as the Great I AM. Remember one of the I AM statements of Jesus was:

Jesus told them,
"I am the bread of life.
Whoever comes to me
will never become hungry,

and whoever believes in me
will never become thirsty."
John 6:35 (GW)

Jesus, The Bread of Life, was and is The Word of God. He willingly fed The Bread of Life to each of His Followers. He commissioned them to do the same for others. Jesus was to share one more meal with His Disciples. He would share breakfast with them by the Sea of Galilee, after His Resurrection.

It is interesting that Jesus shared The Last Supper symbolically as a sunset meal. When He shared the next meal with them, after His Resurrection, it was breakfast, symbolic of sunrise. It was indeed a meal celebrating "Son Rise!"

Following that meal, Jesus commissioned Peter to feed His Word to others.

After they had eaten breakfast, Jesus asked Simon Peter,
"Simon, son of John, do you love me more than the other disciples do?"
Peter answered him, "Yes, Lord, you know that I love you."
Jesus told him, "Feed my lambs."

Jesus asked him again, a second time,
"Simon, son of John, do you love me?"

Peter answered him, "Yes, Lord, you know that I love you."
Jesus told him, "Take care of my sheep."

Jesus asked him a third time,
"Simon, son of John, do you love me?"
Peter felt sad because Jesus had asked him a third time, "Do you love me?"
So Peter said to him, "Lord, you know everything. You know that I love you."
Jesus told him, "Feed my sheep."
John 21:15-17 (GW)

Who gives their whole body for the use of another human being? When a woman is pregnant, her body is no longer exclusively her own. She gives her body in order for another human being to grow. There is no time at any moment of the pregnancy when the mother and baby will be separated. They are together from the first seconds of the pregnancy until the baby is born.

I believe Jesus was referencing the Spiritual Womb relationship when He spoke of giving His Body. He fed the disciples bread. He nurtured them. He was pleased to have given and continue to give His Body for their growth in The Kingdom. He wanted His Disciples to remember what He said to them when they came to Him with the problem of hungry people.

Jesus replied, "You give them something to eat."…
Mark 6:37 (GW)

Then Jesus had magnified the loaves and fishes they had, and allowed the disciples to feed the people. In these final moments of The Last Supper, Jesus called attention to the manner in which The One had already given His Spiritual Body to feed them. He no doubt reminded them of being in the vine. Apart from The One, the disciples would have nothing for themselves to eat and nothing to feed anyone else.

They needed to stay in The Spiritual Womb and keep growing!

Chapter 3

Water, Wine and Blood

*A*t the Last Supper, Jesus gave His Disciples something to drink. Jesus had earlier spoken about a type of water that would never leave anyone thirsty.

> *"But those who drink the water that I will give them*
> *will never become thirsty again.*
> *In fact, the water I will give them will become in them*
> *a spring that gushes up to eternal life."*
> John 4:14 (GW)

So we might think of Jesus offering a pitcher of nice, cold water. But no, what He offered was wine. Jesus referred to it as His Blood. He directed His Disciples to drink it.

> *Then he took a cup and spoke a prayer of thanksgiving.*
> *He gave it to them and said,*
> *"Drink from it, all of you.*
> *This is my blood, the blood of the promise.*
> *It is poured out for many people*
> *so that sins are forgiven."*
> Matthew 26:27-28 (GW)

That sounds really strange. What could Jesus possibly have meant? Is there a connection between water, wine and blood? Yes, but it takes looking beyond the surface to see how interwoven they are. Let's first look at John's revelation.

> *This Son of God is Jesus Christ, who came by water and blood.*
> *He didn't come with water only, but with water and with blood.*
> *The Spirit is the one who verifies this, because the Spirit is the truth.*
> *There are three witnesses: the Spirit, the water, and the blood.*
> *These three witnesses agree.*
> *1 John 5:6-8 (GW)*

This sounds very much like The Three in One, Who always agree! We might think of God representing Water, Jesus representing The Blood and The Holy Spirit representing The Spirit.

Water

There are hundreds of references to water in the Bible. The first mention of water is found in the Book of Genesis, Chapter 1, Verse 2. The last mention is found in Revelation, Chapter 22, Verse 17. Between these two scriptures, water literally flows through the Bible.

God created the sea. He created numerous sea creatures that live in water. Many of them serve as food. In fact, Jesus Himself knew how to fish and after His Resurrection even cooked a breakfast of fish for His Disciples.

Water carried boats, and thus served as an important means of transportation. Even though the creation story demonstrates water can be a divider, it was also a connector after boats began to be used for travel.

Water was used to demonstrate God's Power to act in response to both disobedience and obedience. When the Pharaoh refused to obey God, God turned the waters of Egypt into blood. When Moses and his followers obeyed God, God parted the waters of the sea. God's children walked through on dry ground. The same waters buried the Egyptian soldiers.

Water was important in the testing of humans. Jonah was redirected through a stormy sea into the mouth of a giant sea creature. A major flood redirected the human race in Noah's time. Peter had a test of faith when he attempted to walk on water.

Water was used for cleansing. Naaman was told to bathe seven times in the Jordan River to be cured of leprosy. Jesus washed His Disciples' feet and encouraged them to wash each other's feet.

John baptized with water. Jesus was baptized by water.

We and other creations of God need water to survive. We drink water. We water our plants.

But even more important is the Pure Spiritual Water God gives those who believe in The One. It comes from inside, where The One lives.

[Jesus said]
"As Scripture says, 'Streams of living water
will flow from deep within the person who believes in me.'"
John 7:38 (GW)

The human physical body needs much water to keep it functioning well. In order for our spirits to thrive, we need The Springs of Living Water inside us to have an unhindered flow. If you are feeling dry spiritually, hear the invitation God gives all of us. John heard it when God revealed that we, His Church, are His Bride. Just as Jesus desired His Church to feed others, He also desires that we invite them to our table to receive the Water of Life.

The Spirit and the bride say, "Come!"
Let those who hear this say, "Come!"
Let those who are thirsty come!
Let those who want the water of life take it as a gift.
Revelation 22:17 (GW)

Water and Wine

There once was another wedding.

Three days later a wedding took place in the city of Cana in Galilee.
Jesus' mother was there.
Jesus and his disciples had been invited too.
When the wine was gone, Jesus' mother said to him,
"They're out of wine."
John 2:1-3 (GW)

His mother told the servers, "Do whatever he tells you."
John 2:5 (GW)

Here's where the story gets really interesting.

Six stone water jars were there.
They were used for Jewish purification rituals.
Each jar held 18 to 27 gallons.

Jesus told the servers, "Fill the jars with water."
The servers filled the jars to the brim.

Jesus said to them,
"Pour some, and take it to the person in charge."
The servers did as they were told.
John 2:6-8 (GW)

Would you have had second thoughts about Jesus using jars that were used for washing, not drinking? This event is described as the first recorded Miracle of Jesus. Through His Actions, He made a powerful statement about His Mission on earth. Remember Jesus' Mission was stated through His Name.

"She will give birth to a son,
and you are to give him the name Jesus,
because he will save his people from their sins."
Matthew 1:21 (NIV2011)

By choosing the jars used for ceremonial cleansing, Jesus was pointing to the act of cleansing. In filling the jars with that which would go inside the body, Jesus was indicating the cleansing that needed to begin on the inside. The type of cleansing He had come to do would never be just a ceremony involving the outside of the body. To fulfill His Mission of saving people from their sins, Jesus would be offering deep inner cleansing.

[On another occasion, Jesus said]
"...First clean the inside of the cups and dishes
so that the outside may also be clean."
Matthew 23:26 (GW)

The master of the banquet tasted the water Jesus had turned into wine. He was amazed. He said, "You have saved the best for now." I'm sure Jesus smiled.

The Blood of Jesus

When we think of The Blood of Jesus, many immediately think of the bleeding that came as a result of the torture of the crucifixion. We might believe the Power of His Blood came from the Blood shed at Calvary.

Because of our familiarity with stories of animal sacrifice in the Old Testament, we might think of Jesus' death as a kind of sacrifice. But God brought something far more powerful than any kind of sacrifice.

God was, is and always shall be LOVE. He came to earth revealed as Jesus to show the depths of that Love. He wanted every one of His Creations to know Him and to know His Love for them.

For I desire mercy, not sacrifice,
and acknowledgment of God rather than burnt offerings.
Hosea 6:6 (NIV2011)

We might be tempted to believe that having the Blood of Jesus sprinkled over us would result in evil passing over us. Jesus' Crucifixion coming right at the time of Passover seemed to reinforce that thought.

But God had something far more magnificent than the Passover in mind. He never intended for us to go into hiding from evil. He never intended for us to use Jesus' Blood as some sort of "evil repellent." God planned to expose evil and defeat it! He wanted us to know Him and through Jesus' Life and Death, He wanted us to feel His Steadfast Love.

Jesus' Blood is not a testimony just to the purity of His Blood. It is a Lasting Testimony to what His Pure Blood can do for us. Would you be willing to give up your sin sick blood for a total exchange of Jesus' Pure Blood?

Chapter 4

Sin: Genetic Disease or Infectious Disease?

*H*umans were created perfectly. We were made in the Image of God. Adam and Eve's sins could not change what God created as perfection. Believing that all humanity was doomed as a result of the sin of Adam and Eve would be to give satan far too much credit.

> *The person who sins will die.*
> *A son will not be punished for his father's sins,*
> *and a father will not be punished for his son's sins.*
> *The righteousness of the righteous person will be his own,*
> *and the wickedness of the wicked person will be his own.*
> *Ezekiel 18:20 (GW)*

We are born into a world full of temptations to evil. What Adam and Eve did was open a door to evil. But they did not force anyone to become evil. Just as Eve could not lay her sin completely on the serpent nor could Adam lay his sin on Eve, so we cannot lay our sins on Adam and Eve.

However, sins of those who went before us and sins of those who are with us today do affect us. And our sins affect those around us. We may have come from the womb pure, but once in the world, we quickly hear the noise of the polluted world. It does not take long for us to forget what we learned in the womb.

It is like awakening to a world of mud puddles and trying to learn to walk without ever falling into one. We might be born clean, but it is almost impossible to stay clean.

> *Therefore, just as sin entered the world through one man,*
> *and death through sin,*
> *and in this way death came to all people, because all sinned ...*
> *Romans 5:12-13 (NIV2011)*

Why did death come to all people? It came, not genetically, but because of choices the people made. Being born into a world where there was so much sin, it was very easy for humans to be tempted into sin. It was very easy to "catch" a spiritual disease that could result in eternal death.

There are some illnesses for which there is no cure except to do a total blood exchange. In such treatment, the person's own blood is totally replaced with another's blood.

Jesus' Blood shed at the cross was a powerful, visual pointer to what He was offering us spiritually. He was offering a total spiritual blood exchange. He was offering to take our sin sick blood and replace it with His Pure Blood.

When Jesus was beaten almost beyond recognition, satan meant it as a wonderful demonstration of how fragile and how human this man was. They cut into his skin with whips and nails. They forced a crown of thorns into his head. He bled profusely.

But all satan had done was to take the wrappings off the Gift of God and expose the Goodness beneath. The Blood of Jesus fell first on those who were tormenting Him. After Jesus' Body was taken to the tomb, the soldiers would still be seeing His Blood on their hands and clothes. His Blood would call to them. And some, like the soldier at the foot of the cross, would exclaim in wonder,

... "Surely this man was the Son of God!"
Mark 15:39 (NIV2011)

But before that day, Jesus and Satan would each be preparing. Let's look in on each of them. Satan is reading some future writing and strategizing. Jesus is communing with God and The Holy Spirit.

Chapter 5

The Holy of Holies

Don't you know that your body is a temple
that belongs to the Holy Spirit?
The Holy Spirit, whom you received from God,
lives in you.
You don't belong to yourselves.
1 Corinthians 6:19 (GW)

Satan knew and he hated The Temples. Now that God had put Jesus in a human body, Jesus was like them. His outside body was a covering for what was inside of Him. Jesus' body was an obstacle to satan's getting to the center of Him, where God lived.

Satan had studied the Temple in Jerusalem over and over again. He knew God often showed what was inside by showing what was outside. Jesus was always telling stories, using physical things to teach about spiritual things. Satan took notes and studied. He knew how the Temple was designed.

A tabernacle was set up.
In its first room were the lampstand
and the table with its consecrated bread;

this was called the Holy Place.
Behind the second curtain was a room called the Most Holy Place,
which had the golden altar of incense
and the gold-covered ark of the covenant.
This ark contained the gold jar of manna,
Aaron's staff that had budded,
and the stone tablets of the covenant.

Above the ark were the cherubim of the Glory,
overshadowing the atonement cover. ...
Hebrews 9:2-5 (NIV2011)

Satan scowled. He remembered once being a guardian cherub for God. People thought he was beautiful. Beauty was overrated. He no longer cared about being beautiful. He only wanted to be powerful.

Not only was it important how the Tabernacle (also called The Temple) was constructed, but it was also important who could go there. That was really the part satan was interested in.

When everything had been arranged like this,
the priests entered regularly into the outer room
to carry on their ministry.
But only the high priest entered the inner room,
and that only once a year,
and never without blood,
which he offered for himself
and for the sins the people had committed in ignorance.
The Holy Spirit was showing by this that
the way into the Most Holy Place had not yet been disclosed
as long as the first tabernacle was still functioning.
Hebrews 9:6-8 (NIV2011)

Satan thought he understood. As long as the first tabernacle was still functioning, the inner room would never be revealed. This was simplicity itself. All he had to do was eliminate the first tabernacle. He was sure that "first tabernacle" was Jesus. If he could eliminate Him, he, satan, could be the first one into the inner room. He could become the High Priest of the people.

Human bodies were interesting, but all in all, pretty frail. Satan knew he could take Jesus. Jesus Himself said,

> " *...The spirit is willing, but the flesh is weak."*
> *Matthew 26:41 (NIV2011)*

Satan wanted to get into that inner room. It was going to be a snap to bring blood. He was going to have The Blood of Jesus!

Satan kept reading. He was glad he had access to Paul's writings. That rebel did not even know yet what he was going to write, but satan was not locked into time. He was able to move back and forth across time.

> *But when Christ came as high priest*
> *of the good things that are now already here,*
> *he went through the greater and more perfect tabernacle*
> *that is not made with human hands,*
> *that is to say, is not a part of this creation.*

> *He did not enter by means of the blood of goats and calves;*
> *but he entered the Most Holy Place once for all by his own blood,*
> *thus obtaining eternal redemption.*
> *The blood of goats and bulls and the ashes of a heifer*
> *sprinkled on those who are ceremonially unclean*
> *sanctify them so that they are outwardly clean.*

How much more, then, will the blood of Christ,
who through the eternal Spirit
offered himself unblemished to God,
cleanse our consciences from acts that lead to death,
so that we may serve the living God!
Hebrews 9:11-14 (NIV2011)

Satan slammed the book. He was following everything until he got to that last part. He was not interested in being cleansed of acts that led to death. Death was his business. Why would he want anyone to escape death? And to do all this just to be back where he started—"that we may serve the living God?" Forget that. Satan reckoned that if he could just get to that inner room, everyone would serve him. He would serve no one, especially God.

Meanwhile, Jesus had concluded supper with His Disciples and headed out to the Garden of Gethsemane. He knew what was about to be required of Him. It was the reason for which He had come. Now He wanted to be sure He was completely aligned with all parts of Himself. Many would soon believe He was separate from God and The Holy Spirit. He wanted to be settled within all parts of Himself and firm on The Mission.

Jesus prayed and He positioned His Disciples to hear Him. It was for their benefit that He spoke.

Chapter 6

Is It Time?

J esus thought back over His Mission to save His People from their sins. He had saved many. Many would be saved. But He was thinking of those who would not be saved.

He thought of those who were "blind guides," teachers of the law. Yet their hearts were so far from the intent of the law. They had used the law to enslave people instead of free them. They were bound in pride to the law instead of praising God for the freedom within its boundaries.

"…Because of your traditions you have destroyed the authority of God's word.
You hypocrites! Isaiah was right when he prophesied about you:

'These people honor me with their lips,
but their hearts are far from me.
Their worship of me is pointless,
because their teachings are rules made by humans.'"
Matthew 15:6-9 (GW)

Jesus thought of His recent entry into Jerusalem. He had seen those who were lost. He had longed to gather them up in Love. As He had seen the life of darkness they would live, He had wept.

Through His Tears, He had said,

> …*"If you, even you,*
> *had only known on this day what would bring you peace—*
> *but now it is hidden from your eyes.*
> *The days will come upon you when your enemies*
> *will build an embankment against you*
> *and encircle you and hem you in on every side.*
> *They will dash you to the ground,*
> *you and the children within your walls.*
> *They will not leave one stone on another,*
> *because you did not recognize the time of God's coming to you."*
> *Luke 19:42-44 (NIV2011)*

Later Jesus had spoken directly to the teachers of the law and the Pharisees. He had been direct, calling them out on their sins. And again, in grief, He told them what they had missed because of their choice.

> *"Jerusalem, Jerusalem,*
> *you who kill the prophets and stone those sent to you,*
> *how often I have longed to gather your children together,*
> *as a hen gathers her chicks under her wings,*
> *and you were not willing."*
> *Matthew 23:37 (NIV2011)*

As Jesus began to pray in the Garden of Gethsemane, He told his disciples,

> … *"My soul is overwhelmed with sorrow to the point of death. …"*
> *Matthew 26:38 (NIV2011)*

Many believed He was overwhelmed at the thought of what was about to happen to Him. Luke notes that He was in such anguish that He sweated drops of blood. This happened after He had prayed,

"Father, if you are willing, take this cup from me;
yet not my will, but yours be done."
An angel from heaven appeared to him and strengthened him.
And being in anguish, he prayed more earnestly,
and his sweat was like drops of blood falling to the ground.
Luke 22:42-44 (NIV2011)

I do not believe Jesus was in anguish for Himself. He knew The Glory awaiting Him.

... He saw the joy ahead of him, so he endured death on the cross
and ignored the disgrace it brought him.
Then he received the highest position in heaven,
the one next to the throne of God.
Hebrews 12:2 (GW)

What then would disturb Jesus so much? He was still thinking of those who had not and would not resist the temptation of satan.

Prior to and also after Jesus' asking that the cup be removed from Him if it were God's Will, He warned His Disciples.

..."Pray that you will not fall into temptation."
Luke 22:40 (NIV2011)

... "Get up and pray so that you will not fall into temptation."
Luke 22:46 (NIV2011)

I believe Jesus was thinking, "Just a little more time ... a little more time to save more of our people, Father."

The Lord isn't slow to do what he promised, as some people think.
Rather, he is patient for your sake. He doesn't want to destroy anyone
but wants all people to have an opportunity to turn to him
and change the way they think and act.
2 Peter 3:9 (GW)

But it was time. The Father, The Son and The Holy Spirit came into complete agreement.

After Jesus said this, he looked toward heaven and prayed:
"Father, the hour has come.
Glorify your Son, that your Son may glorify you."
John 17:1 (NIV2011)

Chapter 7

Jesus — The High Priest

The question is frequently raised of whether Jesus really suffered as a fully human person would do. Yes, He did. God, Whose Ways are higher than our ways, deliberately made Himself small enough to suffer for us.

In order to break the law of sin and death, Jesus Himself had to die. From the beginning, satan had worked to blur the lines between good and evil. He worked to make good appear evil and evil to appear good. He attempted to jerk humans back and forth between good and evil so fast they were not sure on which side they should stand.

The events surrounding the crucifixion of Jesus would demonstrate the full power of satan's arsenal of evil. It would demonstrate clearly what the consequences of sin looked like. It would preview graphically what hell would be. It would reveal up close and personal what death looked like.

It would also show what complete obedience to God meant. It would reveal how dark the world can get when one is carrying a load of sin. It would cause all to wonder how a human could endure horrible suffering without crying out to God or ultimately crying out against God.

Jesus would stand before every evil force as The Revealed Temple of The Holy Spirit. It was fitting that satan and his demons would get to cut away the outer wrappings of The Gift God was giving. It was just the beginning of what satan intended for evil being revealed as God's Good Gifts. Soon The Temple would be completely opened to all who wanted to partake of God's Gift of Mercy and Love. Satan would not be inside by his choice.

Since all of these sons and daughters have flesh and blood,
Jesus took on flesh and blood to be like them.
He did this so that by dying he would destroy the one
who had power over death (that is, the devil).
In this way he would free those who were slaves all their lives
because they were afraid of dying.
Hebrews 2:14-15 (GW)

For this reason he had to be made like them,
fully human in every way,
in order that he might become a merciful and faithful high priest
in service to God,
and that he might make atonement for the sins of the people.
Because he himself suffered when he was tempted,
he is able to help those who are being tempted.
Hebrews 2:17-18 (NIV2011)

What could satan do with this exposure of his evil ways? The same thing satan always does. If he cannot get us to believe evil is evil, then his next move is to blame someone other than himself. Satan would be able to deceive many into believing that what Jesus went through is what God would really like to do to them as punishment for being "bad."

Satan would further tempt many to believe God was separate from Jesus. They would believe God sent Jesus to be a public example of what He would do to us, if we didn't "straighten up and fly right."

Isaiah foretold what people would think.

> *He certainly has taken upon himself*
> *our suffering and carried our sorrows,*
> *but we thought that God had wounded him,*
> *beat him, and punished him.*
> *Isaiah 53:4 (GW)*

In the Temple, the Mercy Seat was atop the Ark of the Covenant. This was a beautiful picture of God's Love, Mercy and Grace. God's Law provided the boundaries of Life and His Mercy and Grace provided us the Way to live an abundant Life within those boundaries.

Now let's listen to Jesus' Prayer in the Garden. Turn to the Gospel of John Chapter 17 and share in His Prayer. Did you know Jesus prayed for you before He went to the cross?

> *"I'm not praying only for them.*
> *I'm also praying for those who will believe in me through their message.*
> *I pray that all of these people continue to have unity*
> *in the way that you, Father, are in me and I am in you.*
> *I pray that they may be united with us*
> *so that the world will believe that you have sent me.*
> *I have given them the glory that you gave me.*
> *I did this so that they are united in the same way we are.*
> *I am in them, and you are in me.*
> *So they are completely united.*
> *In this way the world knows that you have sent me*
> *and that you have loved them in the same way you have loved me.*

> *"Father, I want those you have given to me to be with me,*
> *to be where I am. I want them to see my glory,*
> *which you gave me because you loved me*
> *before the world was made.*

Righteous Father, the world didn't know you. Yet, I knew you,
and these {disciples} have known that you sent me.
I have made your name known to them,
and I will make it known so that the love you have
for me will be in them and I will be in them."
John 17:20-26 (GW)

Chapter 8

The Cross: Satan's Perspective

atan was sure he had God backed into a corner. He knew how fragile the human body was. He knew to what lengths the average human would go in order to protect that fragile external covering of what was inside of them.

Satan made it his focused mission to bring suffering to the human body for one important reason. He knew what many humans did not. I'm sure satan hated to even think of Paul, once known as Saul, when he was in satan's army. Saul was to leave him and then actively work against him. Paul was to reveal one of the true secrets of the universe. But Paul had not yet written his epistles in Jesus' day. Satan was hoping he would have time before the secret was revealed.

Don't you know that your body is a temple that belongs to the Holy Spirit?
The Holy Spirit, whom you received from God, lives in you.
You don't belong to yourselves. You were bought for a price.
So bring glory to God in the way you use your body.
1 Corinthians 6:19-20 (GW)

Satan knew the humans had an outside covering they called the human body. It was fragile and fairly easy to conquer. Satan had a regular arsenal of things he could do to the external body, but it was not so easy to get past the inner wall these creatures had. Inside them sat The One. Satan didn't really care that much about any human. He wanted to get inside and defeat The One. If he could force God out of His Own Temple, satan knew the world would be his to command.

But he could never enter the inner court, unless the human let him in. Satan was convinced if he ramped up the external suffering, and the humans believed God would not save them, he would be home free. After all, these humans had to know, God could have prevented their suffering, or at the very least stopped it. Satan's first step was to get these humans to curse God and give up on His Provision.

(satan speaking to God)
"Skin for skin!" Satan replied.
"A man will give all he has for his own life.
But now stretch out your hand and strike his flesh and bones,
and he will surely curse you to your face."
Job 2:4-5 (NIV2011)

Satan wanted humans to fear death. The fear of death drove them to do unimaginable things for him. He cringed the day he heard Jesus tell His Followers:

Don't be afraid of those who kill the body but cannot kill the soul.
Instead, fear the one who can destroy both body and soul in hell.
Matthew 10:28 (GW)

Satan liked the idea of humans being afraid of him. But he wanted them to fear his killing their external body. He really didn't like them knowing anything else. He would love to see them in hell, but only when he was done with them on earth.

When satan was given the opportunity of a lifetime to attack Jesus' Body, he thought his day of triumph had come. If he could bring every torture possible against Jesus' Body, he knew he could demonstrate how fragile that body was.

Satan was sure he could get Jesus to cry out against God and beg for mercy from satan.

Best of all, apparently God planned this fight of the ages to be very public. Satan liked that. He could imagine the cheers of the crowd already, as he would do his victory dance on what would be left of the Body of Jesus.

Satan planned his attack on Jesus. He knew from his experiments with humans how important it was to get them in the right frame of mind. A good dose of rejection was the way to start.

He contemplated getting Jesus' Followers to argue over petty things, like who would be the greatest in the kingdom. That should cause Jesus to doubt whether He had gotten through to these men at all. Maybe he could get some of Jesus' trusted Followers to reject Him by betraying Him, denying Him, doubting Him and completely abandoning Him.

Surely that would get Jesus in the right frame of mind to feel alone and rejected. But satan was just getting started. What if he could get that crowd, who seemed to love Him, to reject Him less than a week later? Yes, that was it. They could cry for Jesus' death, while calling for a criminal to be released. Yes, Jesus was big on justice. Satan was sure he could weaken Jesus with a combined dose of rejection with injustice.

Satan put his most trusted demons on the case and all went as planned. Satan watched as his faithful guard beat Jesus so badly, He was not even recognizable. He listened for Jesus to cry for mercy. He listened for Jesus to curse God. But He said nothing.

Satan slithered along and watched Jesus walk to Golgotha. Jesus carried that cross beam on his shoulders right past those who were supposed to love Him. But no one lifted a finger to save Him. Even His Mother looked upon Him and did nothing. Satan was pleased. It was appropriately humiliating, painful, and unjust.

Then the soldiers hung Jesus on the cross. Satan thought it was kind of ironic that Jesus had spent His younger days working with wood as a carpenter. Then He came to the end of his life, nailed to wood. Again satan laughed. "Guess you're on the wrong side of the hammer now, Jesus. Watch your hands!"

He was up there between two thieves. Satan had handpicked them. Jesus had called him a thief.

> *"The thief comes only to steal and kill and destroy; …"*
> *John 10:10 (NIV2011)*

So satan thought it only fitting that he assure Jesus understand what it was like to be in the company of thieves. One of them faithfully carried out his mission and flung insults at Jesus. Satan was proud. More rejection would assure that Jesus realize how far He had fallen.

Satan didn't know how to account for the other thief. He defected at the last minute and wanted to go with Jesus into His Kingdom. Satan didn't understand him anymore than he understood Jesus. Jesus accepted satan's defector and took him with Him.

Jesus suffered. It was everything satan hoped for. His favorite part was when it got really dark. He did his best work in the dark. It stayed dark for a long time. Satan took this as a sign that God recognized that darkness could conquer His Light. Everyone saw it! It was the highpoint of a really great day, especially when Jesus seemed to give His One and Only Statement that sounded like He was giving up.

> *" …My God, my God, why have you forsaken me?"*
> *Matthew 27:46 (NIV2011)*

He seemed to be asking God if He had forsaken Him. That was great! Satan knew it could not happen, but still … just the fact that He said it was fantastic.

He knew people would remember that line forever. However this thing turned out, that was a real victory.

When satan tells the story, he likes to end things at the cross. Long after many others had left, satan was still there. He gazed in admiration at the pathetic body of Jesus. He took delight in believing that Jesus' last words had been a clear statement of what he, satan wanted to tell the world. God has forsaken you!

Satan looked in wonder at the world he believed would be his to command shortly. He slithered back and forth in the pools of blood that had not dried yet. And he wondered what that sweet smell was.

Chapter 9

Satan Waits At The Cross ...

hile Satan waited for what he believed would be the end of Jesus, he reminisced with some of his demon underlings. Satan had been delighted to have such a fortunate opportunity with Eve. His techniques had worked well. If he had only been able to get Adam and Eve to eat of the Tree of Life and live forever, he would have had plenty of time to perfect everything.

But that had been just a temporary setback. Even though God bounced them all out of the garden, there had been other chances for satan to advance his evil plans. Satan was patient.

> *When the devil had finished all this tempting,*
> *he left him until an opportune time.*
> *Luke 4:13 (NIV2011)*

There had been plenty of opportune times. Satan had managed to get quite a few people on his payroll. He always used his proven formula.

Plant doubt. Make the human doubt what God said. Make the human believe God has not provided as much as He could have. Offer them what they believe they have missed. Promise them anything. Capture them. Put them on the payroll for the wages of sin. Keep them working for you. If they try to defect, heap lots of guilt and shame on them. Convince them God will never take them back. Threaten them with horrible things if they try to leave.

Satan made it clear to his demon lieutenants they were never to permit the humans to start thanking God for anything. If they somehow slipped through and did, the demons were to negate every positive thought with a negative one. Satan still wasn't sure what had gone wrong in the bronze snake incident.

He had succeeded in getting the people to complain bitterly about what God had provided for them. He was sure he had them. Yet somehow God had turned the tables on him. When he saw Moses lifting the bronze snake, he was sure victory was within his grasp. But it somehow backfired.

Satan reckoned maybe it had something to do with the humans asking forgiveness. He had to admit he didn't understand the concept of forgiveness. It didn't make sense. It seemed so weak.

Satan took another victory slither around the cross. He smugly patted himself on the head with his tail. It had been a really good day. He had absolutely perfected his attacks on the human body. He had to hand it to Jesus. He had suffered quietly, like a lamb being led to the slaughter. Satan was surprised. He expected more from Him. Even though the torture was pretty dramatic, a good show of resistance would have made it better.

Speaking of sweet, satan wondered again where that sweet smell was coming from. He had been to plenty of crucifixions. He had never smelled anything like that. It reminded him of that expensive perfume.

Satan thought about that bronze snake episode again. Jesus had said something really strange about it recently. Satan, like any good scout for the other team, had watched Jesus every minute. He had taken mental notes on everything Jesus said, so he could incorporate it into his plans. What could Jesus have meant when he said,

"Just as Moses lifted up the snake in the wilderness,
so the Son of Man must be lifted up,
that everyone who believes may have eternal life in him."
John 3:14-15 (NIV2011)

Satan had a moment of doubt himself. He hated it. He was not used to having any doubts about anything. Had he missed something?

But wait, no, all was well. He thought Jesus was too far gone to say anything else, but Jesus was speaking. Satan leaned in to hear His weak Voice.

But ... The Voice was not weak. It was as if every roll of thunder satan had ever heard was combined into one mighty drum roll.

..."It is finished!" ...
John 19:30 (GW)

Chapter 10

Jubilee Day!

*S*atan was still rejoicing at Jesus' Words of "My God, My God, why have you forsaken Me?" Satan was not quite the Bible scholar he believed himself to be. If he had recalled The Book of Psalms, Chapter 22, he would have realized Jesus was quoting the lament of a hurting and grieving person. He was making a statement for all humanity who are weighed down with so many sins, they can no longer see God's Face.

The Book of Psalms, Chapter 22 is a lament. But it ends with the triumphant Message that was about to be revealed from the cross.

> *Posterity will serve him;*
> *future generations will be told about the Lord.*
> *They will proclaim his righteousness,*
> *declaring to a people yet unborn:*
> *He has done it!*
> *Psalm 22:30-31 (NIV2011)*

At the moment satan heard those words, "It is finished," he felt relieved. His plans had gone like clockwork. He interpreted Jesus' proclamation as the beginning of Jesus' concession speech.

But it was Jesus' next Words that changed everything completely.

Jesus called out with a loud voice,
"Father, into your hands I commit my spirit." ...
Luke 23:46 (NIV2011)

We describe The Resurrection as happening on the third day after Jesus died on the cross. I believe that in fact, the True Resurrection happened at the moment Jesus dismissed His Spirit to God and The Holy Spirit. The Power of The Three in One was felt throughout the earth, including what was about to become a very shaky earth for satan.

At that moment
the curtain of the temple was torn in two from top to bottom.
The earth shook, the rocks split and the tombs broke open.
The bodies of many holy people who had died were raised to life.
They came out of the tombs after Jesus' resurrection
and went into the holy city and appeared to many people.

When the centurion and those with him
who were guarding Jesus saw the earthquake
and all that had happened, they were terrified, and exclaimed,
"Surely he was the Son of God!"
Matthew 27:51-54 (NIV2011)

I like to imagine that something else very significant was happening in the world of the Spirit. The One surrounded satan and said, "We have come to receive the wages you owe our people. We are here to settle the books."

Satan said, "You can't accept the wages for other people. They worked for me. They earned what they earned. Only they can receive their wages. That's the rule. You always go by the book. So you know what's legal and what is not. I am in charge of the book of death. No one can open it but me."

God's Words are timeless. We are benefiting from Words spoken long ago. We speak and hear Words today. God allows us to hear Words now that will not be revealed to others until some time in the future. I believe satan may have heard the words John later heard in his Revelation from God.

> *"...I am the first and the last, the living one.*
> *I was dead, but now I am alive forever.*
> *I have the keys of death and hell."*
> *Revelation 1:17-18 (GW)*

I believe satan's protests were drowned out by the voices of angels and saints of God, who attested to The Power and Authority of The One to receive and deal with satan's payroll.

> *And they sang a new song, saying:*
> *"You are worthy to take the scroll*
> *and to open its seals,*
> *because you were slain,*
> *and with your blood you purchased for God*
> *persons from every tribe and language and people and nation.*
> *You have made them to be a kingdom and priests to serve our God,*
> *and they will reign on the earth."*

> *Then I looked and heard the voice of many angels,*
> *numbering thousands upon thousands and ten thousand times ten thousand.*
> *They encircled the throne and the living creatures and the elders.*
> *In a loud voice they were saying:*

> *"Worthy is the Lamb, who was slain,*
> *to receive power and wealth and wisdom and strength*
> *and honor and glory and praise!"*
> *Then I heard every creature in heaven and on earth and under the earth and*
> *on the sea, and all that is in them, saying:*

"To him who sits on the throne and to the Lamb
be praise and honor and glory and power,
for ever and ever!"
Revelation 5:9-13 (NIV2011)

Satan tried one last plea. "They can't be forgiven. They haven't asked You. They haven't forgiven anyone. I know Your Rules."

I believe The One told satan, "You have spoken wrongly. This is the moment of The Jubilee! No longer will it be limited to once every seven years or to a specific day on the calendar.

On this day at this time, all debts are forgiven. All those held captive by you are freed. All property and everything I have given them from the beginning are returned to them. And from this day forward, it shall be that when they ask for the Mercy of The Jubilee, I will give it to them."

Satan saw The One, standing in Power and Authority. He became aware of being sprinkled with fresh blood and water, gushing from the side of Jesus. And he heard,

This is the one who came by water and blood—Jesus Christ.
He did not come by water only, but by water and blood.
And it is the Spirit who testifies, because the Spirit is the truth.
For there are three that testify: the Spirit, the water and the blood;
and the three are in agreement.
1 John 5:6-8 (NIV2011)

Chapter 11

One Time Gift OR Perpetual Gift?

*A*s we have discussed in previous chapters, Jesus gave Gifts of Forgiveness and Healing to people who did not specifically ask for those Gifts. He acted out of Compassion and Mercy.

There was no doubt He had Authority to forgive sins and heal. He was willing to forgive sins and heal. He healed them all, not some, but all. He does not desire that anyone perish, but that all might come to salvation.

The key factor was whether they were willing to receive what God had for them, once He removed all barriers.

On "Jubilee Day," I believe The Gift of Salvation was offered to all. All sins were forgiven, satan's slaves were set free and all property taken by satan was returned to its rightful owner. All God had intended for everyone to have from the beginning of their life was legally theirs once again.

However, what happened next was up to them. They had received a monumental Gift with a welcoming invitation to get to truly know The One … to know Him as The Lord of Love, Mercy and Grace. It was an invitation not only to experience Abundant Life, but also Eternal Life.

However, satan would recover from his loss at the cross. He would dust himself off (which would be hard to do, since he was spending a lot of time slithering in the dust). He would begin again with scheming and planning how to conquer humans. Some who had received God's Gifts would relinquish them and return to satan's dark side.

In the original system of Jubilee, they would have to wait at least seven years for their freedom from debt and slavery and fifty years to get their property back. However, in the new system, spiritual freedom would be offered at anytime.

God, living inside each and every one of His Creations, continued to call from the insides of them where He lived. They would continue to be His Temples, even when the lights were turned out. Some would only see the outside of themselves, never knowing who God created them to be.

Some would only get to the outer room of their Temple and would be content to live and work from there, even calling themselves Christians. But they would never go inside to the Holy of Holies, and claim eternal life by getting to know The One Who was waiting for them there.

Some would remember the Joy they experienced on Jubilee Day when they went all the way inside into the arms of The One, Who was waiting to welcome them Home. They would do life, from that moment on, from the inner room with The One.

"You will seek me and find me
when you seek me with all your heart."
Jeremiah 29:13 (NIV2011)

Do you not know that you are the temple of God
and that the Spirit of God dwells in you?
1 Corinthians 3:16 (NKJV)

But Christ is faithful as the Son over God's house.
And we are his house,
if indeed we hold firmly to our confidence
and the hope in which we glory.
Hebrews 3:6 (NIV2011)

... the glorious riches of this mystery,
which is Christ in you,
the hope of glory.
Colossians 1:27 (NIV2011)

Through him you, also, are being built in the Spirit
together with others into a place where God lives.
Ephesians 2:22 (GW)

Jesus answered him, "Those who love me will do what I say.
My Father will love them,
and we will go to them and make our home with them."
John 14:23 (GW)

Guard the good deposit that was entrusted to you—
guard it with the help of the Holy Spirit who lives in us.
2 Timothy 1:14 (NIV2011)

"This is eternal life:
to know you, the only true God,
and Jesus Christ, whom you sent."
John 17:3 (GW)

Chapter 12

Jesus, Is It Really You?

*J*esus was definitely dead. The Roman soldiers made sure of that. He was placed in a tomb and a huge stone placed in front of it. Additionally, there was a guard posted to be sure His Body was not stolen.

On the third day of the week, very early in the morning, the women who were among Jesus' Followers, went to His Tomb. They took spices, intending to complete the burial routine. However, the stone that had blocked the way into the tomb was rolled away.

Rarely is it discussed how those women thought they were going to gain access to the tomb, had the stone been in place. But perhaps the answer is simply faith. They knew God would provide whatever they needed to do the task to which they were called. And He did!

Finding no stone blocking their way, the women entered the tomb. There were more surprises. There was no body in the tomb. While the women were trying to figure out what had happened,

… suddenly two men in clothes that gleamed like lightning stood beside them.

In their fright the women bowed down with their faces to the ground,
but the men said to them,
"Why do you look for the living among the dead?
He is not here; he is risen! ..."
Luke 24:4-6 (NIV2011)

The women ran back to the men and told them what had happened. The men did not believe them. Peter ran to the tomb to check it out himself. He found the grave clothes lying by themselves, but he saw no body, either living or dead.

In spite of Jesus' telling them ahead of time that He would die and rise again, they seemed baffled. How often we are in the same position. God tells us something. We say we believe it, but then we act as if we do not believe it. Sometimes we look and see The Truth and are even able to verbalize The Truth, but we don't absorb The Truth. Such was the case with Mary, who remained at the tomb, even after everyone else had gone.

The Gardener?

Now Mary stood outside the tomb crying.
As she wept, she bent over to look into the tomb
and saw two angels in white, seated where Jesus' body had been,
one at the head and the other at the foot.

They asked her, "Woman, why are you crying?"

"They have taken my Lord away," she said,
"and I don't know where they have put him."
At this, she turned around and saw Jesus standing there,
but she did not realize that it was Jesus.

He asked her, "Woman, why are you crying?
Who is it you are looking for?"

Thinking he was the gardener, she said,

"Sir, if you have carried him away,
tell me where you have put him and I will get him."

Jesus said to her, "Mary." …
John 20:11-16 (NIV2011)

No one had ever said her name with as much Love as Jesus. When He spoke her name, there could be no doubt that it was He. I like to believe that perhaps two other pieces of information Jesus had already spoken came to mind.

"…He who has seen me has seen the Father. …"
John 14:9 (NIV2014)

"I am the true vine, and my Father is the gardener."
John 15:1 (NIV2011)

Mary had been right. She did see The Gardener!

<u>He walked and talked with them!</u>
That same day, two of Jesus' Followers were going to a village called Emmaus. They were talking about everything that had happened. As they were walking and talking, Jesus Himself came up and walked along with them. However, they did not recognize Him. This is much the same as today. The One walks with us every moment and yet we don't recognize Him.

Jesus asked them what they were talking about. They told Him. He chided them for not believing what had already been foretold.

He said to them,
"How foolish you are,
and how slow to believe all that the prophets have spoken!
Did not the Messiah have to suffer these things

and then enter his glory?"
And beginning with Moses and all the Prophets,
he explained to them what was said
in all the Scriptures concerning himself.
Luke 24:25-27 (NIV2011)

Again, how like us. We walk with Him. He talks to us. He reminds us of all that has been written and spoken about Him. Still we do not recognize that He is with us at this moment.

As they approached the village, it appeared Jesus was going to keep going. But they did not want Him to leave. They asked Him to stay for the night. When we are in the Presence of God, we often do not recognize it … and yet when we sense that Presence moving away from us, something in our heart yearns for Him to stay.

Jesus agreed.

<u>He ate with them!</u>

When he was at the table with them,
he took bread, gave thanks, broke it and began to give it to them.
Then their eyes were opened and they recognized him,
and he disappeared from their sight.
They asked each other, "Were not our hearts burning within us
while he talked with us on the road
and opened the Scriptures to us?"
Luke 24:30-32 (NIV2011)

They immediately returned to Jerusalem, declaring it was true that The Lord had risen. How many encounters have you had with the Risen Jesus? Stop now and remember the events of your life. Are there times now, looking back, you realize you were in The Presence of The Lord and did not recognize Him?

Life got more amazing with each moment.

> *While they were still talking about this,*
> *Jesus himself stood among them and said to them,*
> *"Peace be with you."*

> *They were startled and frightened, thinking they saw a ghost.*
> *He said to them,*
> *"Why are you troubled, and why do doubts rise in your minds?*
> *Look at my hands and my feet.*
> *It is I myself!*
> *Touch me and see;*
> *a ghost does not have flesh and bones, as you see I have."*

> *When he had said this, he showed them his hands and feet.*
> *And while they still did not believe it because of joy and amazement,*
> *he asked them,*
> *"Do you have anything here to eat?"*
> *They gave him a piece of broiled fish,*
> *and he took it and ate it in their presence.*
> *Luke 24:36-43 (NIV2011)*

He told the Truth!

Jesus was fully demonstrating that what He had told them in Truth was still True. He presented Himself as very solid evidence of Life. He had all the Parts of His Body, He was able to walk and talk, and He was definitely the same Jesus, Who loved to eat! But something was different. He seemed to be able to travel place to place and appear and disappear. Yes, something was definitely different.

> *He said to them,*
> *"This is what I told you while I was still with you:*
> *Everything must be fulfilled that is written about me*
> *in the Law of Moses, the Prophets and the Psalms."*

Then he opened their minds so they could understand the Scriptures.
He told them, "This is what is written:
The Messiah will suffer and rise from the dead on the third day,
and repentance for the forgiveness of sins will be preached in his name
to all nations, beginning in Jerusalem.
You are witnesses of these things.
I am going to send you what my Father has promised;
but stay in the city
until you have been clothed with power from on high."
Luke 24:44-49 (NIV2011)

Do you believe what Jesus said about Himself, God and The Holy Spirit? Are you seeking Him? Where are you looking? Don't look for The Living among the Dead. You will not find Him there.

He has risen, just as He said!

Chapter 13

Alive Forever More!

*J*esus remained on earth for approximately forty days before He ascended into heaven. He had prepared His Followers for the day they would no longer see Him in one physical body. He would continue His Work, with God, The Holy Spirit and His Followers in a home base He had revealed to them. He would be working from the inside of their bodies.

Satan had a monumental problem. He had thrown everything he had at Jesus, believing he could destroy Jesus' Temple and gain access to the inner courts from which he could rule. But it hadn't happened.

Satan was forced to review everything in an effort to determine where he had gone wrong. He began by reviewing everything Jesus had said about the temple. He was sure Jesus' description of earthly things would reveal something about the spiritual world.

He remembered that day Jesus had cleared the temple of those doing business. Jesus had accused them of turning His Father's house into a market. Not only were Jesus' actions against legitimate businessmen an outrage, but He even called the temple His Father's House, flaunting His Kinship with God.

Satan smiled to remember how angry the people were with Jesus. He had enjoyed every minute of Jesus having a major meltdown.

The Jews then responded to him,
"What sign can you show us to prove your authority to do all this?"
Jesus answered them,
"Destroy this temple, and I will raise it again in three days."
John 2:18-19 (NIV2011)

The people thought he was a mad man. Satan agreed.

They replied, "It has taken forty-six years to build this temple,
and you are going to raise it in three days?"
John 2:20 (NIV2011)

Satan suddenly had a moment of clarity. The realization made him sick.

But the temple he had spoken of was his body.
After he was raised from the dead,
his disciples recalled what he had said.
Then they believed the scripture and
the words that Jesus had spoken.
John 2:21-22 (NIV2011)

"OK, OK," Satan thought. "So Jesus had risen from the dead. Big deal. He had His fun for forty more days. Now He could go home and leave everyone on earth alone. Another forty days and this whole thing would blow over." Satan stretched out in the sun to take a nap.

As he drifted off to sleep, he had another thought. Jesus would be ascending to His Father. That was great! The people would think both God and Jesus were in heaven. He knew the humans didn't know where heaven was, but they believed it was a long way from where they were. Separation of God and Jesus from the humans—it was everything satan wanted.

Would Jesus really go off and leave His Followers? Was Heaven really that far away? Jesus had told His Followers The Plan, even before He went to the cross.

> " *…For indeed, the kingdom of God is within you.*"
> *Luke 17:21 (NKJV)*

> "*I will not leave you all alone. <u>I will come back to you.</u>*
> *In a little while the world will no longer see me,*
> *<u>but you will see me. You will live because I live,</u>*
> *On that day you will know that*
> *<u>I am in my Father and that you are in me and that I am in you.</u>*
> *Whoever knows and obeys my commandments is the person who loves me.*
> *Those who love me will have my Father's love,*
> *and <u>I, too, will love them and show myself to them.</u>*"
> *John 14:18-21 (GW)*
> *(Underline added for emphasis)*

Satan awakened to new information coming in. God's Plan was not a secret. Jesus' Followers were openly talking about all He had said to them. Satan was immediately thrown back into "damage control" mode again. He called an emergency meeting of all his demons.

His first choice would have been that no one ever consider the possibility that Jesus could come back in any form. He admitted he could not do much about Jesus' immediate Followers remembering His Words. But satan was sure he could affect the message going out to those in future generations.

Satan told his demons, "Be sure everyone but Jesus' Disciples knows that His Words were only for Jesus' Disciples. If you find anyone who believes Jesus' Words are for them, let them. But be sure they know they will have to wait a long time for Jesus to get back with them. When they are wallowing in their misery, pat them on the back, give a deep sigh, and say, 'Just wait, Jesus will be back one day.' And oh yeah, one more thing—keep them busy while they wait!"

What should we remember? Jesus' Words are true and can be trusted. Satan is a liar.

When Jesus rose into the clouds on His Day of Ascension, He did not leave a Parting Promise. He left an Imparting Promise. And He wanted us to be absolutely certain we understood.

> *When Jesus came near, he spoke to them. He said,*
> *"All authority in heaven and on earth has been given to me.*
> *So wherever you go, make disciples of all nations:*
> *Baptize them in the name of the Father, and of the Son,*
> *and of the Holy Spirit.*
> *Teach them to do everything I have commanded you.*
> *"And remember that I am always with you until the end of time."*
> *Matthew 28:18-20 (GW)*

Jesus started His Message early in His Ministry when He met the woman at the well. She believed in God. She believed there would be a time when The Messiah would be revealed. Her mistake was that she was looking off into the future for The Messiah when He was standing right in front of her. Don't make the same mistake of waiting to see Jesus at the Second Coming. He is here now, in Full Power and Authority, waiting for us to join Him in the Ongoing Mission!

What about that special event that many refer to as Jesus' Second Coming? God, Jesus and The Holy Spirit will continue to come to all peoples on earth, not just at some future time, but also now at this time. They will work together in various ways and always with the same goal.

They are seeking the lost and wanting to bring them Home. They are seeking those in darkness and turning on The Lights. They are waiting for everyone to open the Gifts they were given from the beginning of their Life and share them with the rest of The Body of Christ.

Some will be won into the Kingdom of Light. Some will remain in the Kingdom of Darkness. However, there will come a day when they can no longer look away from The Light. They will see! They will bow! They will proclaim The Name of Jesus!

"Look, he is coming with the clouds,"
and every eye will see him,
even those who pierced him";
and all peoples on earth "will mourn because of him."
So shall it be! Amen.
Revelation 1:7 (NIV2011)

…that at the name of Jesus every knee should bow,
in heaven and on earth and under the earth,
and every tongue acknowledge that Jesus Christ is Lord,
to the glory of God the Father.
Philippians 2:10-11 (NIV2011)

Chapter 14

Clouds — Looking at Both Sides Now

*A*ccording to dictionary.com, a cloud is "a visible collection of particles of water or ice suspended in the air, usually at an elevation above the earth's surface."

David the Psalmist observed:

> *The heavens declare the glory of God,*
> *and the sky displays what his hands have made.*
> *One day tells a story to the next.*
> *One night shares knowledge with the next without talking,*
> *without words, without their voices being heard.*
> *{Yet,} their sound has gone out into the entire world,*
> *their message to the ends of the earth. …*
> *Psalm 19:1-4 (GW)*

God frequently speaks through His Heavens.

After the Great Flood, God established His Covenant with the people of earth, giving as His Reassuring Sign, a rainbow in the clouds.

"I have set my rainbow in the clouds,
and it will be the sign of the covenant between me and the earth."
Genesis 9:13 (NIV2011)

When God led His People out of Egypt, He did so with a pillar of cloud by day and a pillar of fire by night.

By day the LORD went ahead of them in a pillar of cloud
to guide them on their way
and by night in a pillar of fire to give them light,
so that they could travel by day or night.
Neither the pillar of cloud by day
nor the pillar of fire by night
left its place in front of the people.
Exodus 13:21-22 (NIV2011)

God appeared in the tabernacle over The Mercy Seat in a cloud, verifying His Presence.

"…for I will appear in the cloud above the mercy seat."
Leviticus 16:2 (NKJV)

God revealed His Glory to His People in the cloud covering The Tent of Meeting.

It came about, however,
when the congregation had assembled against Moses and Aaron,
that they turned toward the tent of meeting,
and behold, the cloud covered it
and the glory of the LORD appeared.
Numbers 16:42 (NASV)

The people of Solomon's day also experienced God's Glory through the cloud.

It happened that when the priests came from the holy place,
the cloud filled the house of the LORD,
so that the priests could not stand to minister because of the cloud,
for the glory of the LORD filled the house of the LORD.
Then Solomon said,
"The LORD has said that He would dwell in the thick cloud."
1 Kings 8:10-12 (NASV)

There are many more references to clouds. Jesus Himself made two references to His Coming in the Clouds. He made the first reference in speaking to His Followers. He made the second reference in speaking to those who were against Him.

"Then will appear the sign of the Son of Man in heaven.
And then all the peoples of the earth will mourn
when they see the Son of Man coming on the clouds of heaven,
with power and great glory."
Matthew 24:30 (NIV2011)

... The high priest said to him,
"I charge you under oath by the living God:
Tell us if you are the Messiah, the Son of God."
"You have said so," Jesus replied.
"But I say to all of you:
From now on you will see the Son of Man
sitting at the right hand of the Mighty One
and coming on the clouds of heaven."
Matthew 26:63-64 (NIV2011)

It is not surprising that satan would want to top Jesus. He wanted to ascend above the clouds.

(satan speaking)
… "I will ascend to the heavens;
I will raise my throne
above the stars of God;
I will sit enthroned on the mount of assembly,
on the upmost heights of Mount Zaphon.
I will ascend above the tops of the clouds;
I will make myself like the Most High."
Isaiah 14:13-14 (NIV2011)

When Jesus ascended, He ascended into The Cloud, where God had revealed Himself and His Glory many times before. When Jesus prayed in the Garden of Gethsemane, He had said

After Jesus said this, he looked toward heaven and prayed:
"Father, the hour has come.
Glorify your Son, that your Son may glorify you."
John 17:1 (NIV2011)

And so Jesus ascended into The Glory!

Now when He had spoken these things,
while they watched, He was taken up,
and a cloud received Him out of their sight.
Acts 1:9 (NKJV)

At the time of the Revelation of Jesus to all people, He will once again make His Grand Entrance in the clouds.

"Look, he is coming with the clouds,"
and "every eye will see him,
even those who pierced him";
and all peoples of earth "will mourn because of him,"
So shall it be! Amen.
Revelation 1:7 (NIV2011)

After that, we who are still alive and are left
will be caught up together with them in the clouds
to meet the Lord in the air.
And so we will be with the Lord forever.
Therefore encourage one another with these words.
1 Thessalonians 4:17-18 (NIV2011)

Paul described the beautiful picture of those Saints of God, who have preceded us in being promoted to Glory. He sees them as a "great cloud of witnesses." He sees them as being in the grandstands with The One, cheering for those of us who are still laboring on earth. What a wonderful reception awaits us when we cross the finish line. The finish line would more aptly be called the "beginning line"!

Therefore, since we are surrounded
by such a great cloud of witnesses,
let us throw off everything that hinders
and the sin that so easily entangles.
And let us run with perseverance the race marked out for us,
fixing our eyes on Jesus, the pioneer and perfecter of faith.
For the joy set before him he endured the cross,
scorning its shame,
and sat down at the right hand of the throne of God.
Consider him who endured such opposition from sinners,
so that you will not grow weary and lose heart.
Hebrews 12:1-3 (NIV2011)

The ONE
in
Us!
The Mission Continues!

"On that day you will realize that
I am in my Father,
and you are in me,
and I am in you."
John 14:20 (NIV2011)

"So wherever you go, make disciples of all nations:
Baptize them in the name of
the Father, and of the Son, and of the Holy Spirit.
Teach them to do everything I have commanded you.
And remember that
I am always with you until the end of time."
Matthew 28:19-20 (GW)

Chapter 1

Do You Want to be a Disciple?

*T*hrough Jesus, God has given us an Amazing Invitation to enter into the center of The Three in One. Many of us would step back from the thought of functioning with God, Jesus and The Holy Spirit. Isn't that putting ourselves on much too high a plain? Are we in danger of having thoughts like satan had?

No, to both questions. Satan was not interested in being in a womb relationship with God. He wanted to ditch everyone but himself. He wanted to replace God, not be in relationship with Him.

We cannot ascend to the heights from which God operates unless He invites us and we accept His Invitation. We are like a small child, who raises our hands to a Loving Father to be picked up. We reach up to Him in trust. He picks us up in Love and shows us the world through His eyes.

He explains His Mission and shows us how we can partner with Him to accomplish it. If we are willing to spend time with Him and listen closely, He will show us things we never knew before.

Call to me, and I will answer you.
I will tell you great and mysterious things that you do not know.
Jeremiah 33:3 (GW)

You will seek me and find me when you seek me with all your heart.
Jeremiah 29:13 (NIV2011)

Many of God's Messages are not hidden. They are right out in the open. He let us know He was "God with us" when He put His Name in Jesus' other Name of Immanuel. Jesus assured us that He and we are in The Father God.

God further verified this for us through the Precious Name of Jesus. Look closely at the name, JESUS. The fourth letter is U. You (U) are in Jesus. He is in you.

You and the rest of His Creations are connected in Him. Go either to the right or to the left from the U and you will discover US.

God has also put instructions for us in His Name. Read the first two words and you will find "Go." Read the third letter and then the second letter and you will find "Do." You will find His complete instructions when you search His Word for the many times He said, "Go!' or "Do!"

Let's look at Jesus' Imparting Words, which include His Command to "GO!"

"So wherever you go, make disciples of all nations:
Baptize them in the name of
the Father, and of the Son, and of the Holy Spirit.
Teach them to do everything I have commanded you.
And remember that I am always with you until the end of time."
Matthew 28:19-20 (GW)

Being Jesus' Disciple is an ongoing process. He continues to make us His Disciples, so we can go and make other people His Disciples. Before we can go, He needs to be assured we really want to be His Disciples. Let's review the "job description" given by Jesus.

Chapter 2

What It Means To Be A Disciple of Jesus

<u>Love God and Everyone He Created.</u>
"Teacher, which commandment is the greatest in Moses' Teachings?"

Jesus answered him,
"'Love the Lord your God with all your heart,
with all your soul, and with all your mind.'
This is the greatest and most important commandment.

The second is like it:
'Love your neighbor as you love yourself.'
All of Moses' Teachings and the Prophets
depend on these two commandments."
Matthew 22:36-40 (GW)

"I'm giving you a new commandment:
Love each other
in the same way that I have loved you.
Everyone will know that you are my disciples
because of your love for each other."
John 13:34-35 (GW)

<u>Forgive.</u>
"For if you forgive other people when they sin against you,
your heavenly Father will also forgive you.
But if you do not forgive others their sins,
your Father will not forgive your sins."
Matthew 6:14-15 (NIV2011)

<u>Don't Judge.</u>
"Do not judge, or you too will be judged.
For in the same way you judge others, you will be judged,
and with the measure you use,
it will be measured to you."
Matthew 7:1-2 (NIV2011)

<u>Don't Have a "Get Even" Mentality.</u>
When the disciples James and John saw this, they asked,
"Lord, do you want us to call fire down from heaven to destroy them?"
But Jesus turned and rebuked them.
Luke 9:54-55 (NIV2011)

"...love your enemies and pray for those who persecute you,
that you may be children of your Father in heaven. ..."
Matthew 5:44-45 (NIV2011)

<u>Take The Higher Road.</u>

"Blessed are you when people insult you,
persecute you, lie, and say all kinds of evil things about you
because of me.
Rejoice and be glad because you have a great reward in heaven!
The prophets who lived before you were persecuted in these ways."
Matthew 5:11-12 (GW)

<u>Enlarge Your Family.</u>
He replied to the man speaking to him,
"Who is my mother, and who are my brothers?"
Pointing with his hand at his disciples, he said,
"Look, here are my mother and my brothers.
Whoever does what my Father in heaven wants
is my brother and sister and mother."
Matthew 12:48-50 (GW)

<u>Be Willing To Leave Your Family.</u>
"And everyone who has left houses or brothers or sisters
or father or mother or wife or children or fields for my sake
will receive a hundred times as much
and will inherit eternal life."
Matthew 19:29 (NIV2011)

… But he replied, "Lord first let me go and bury my father."
Jesus said to him, "Let the dead bury their own dead,
but you go and proclaim the kingdom of God."
Luke 9:59-60 (NIV2011)

"Anyone who loves their father or mother more than me
is not worthy of me;
anyone who loves their son or daughter more than me
is not worthy of me."
Matthew 10:37 (NIV2011)

<u>Be Willing To Give Up All Your Earthly Possessions.</u>
Jesus told him, "Foxes have holes, and birds have nests,
but the Son of Man has nowhere to sleep."
Luke 9:58 (GW)

Jesus looked at him and loved him.
"One thing you lack," he said.
"Go, sell everything you have and give to the poor,
and you will have treasure in heaven.
Then come, follow me."
Mark 10:21 (NIV2011)

Experience Grace Personally.
[Paul said] ... I was given a thorn in my flesh,
a messenger of Satan, to torment me.
Three times I pleaded with the Lord to take it away from me.
But he said to me,
"My grace is sufficient for you,
for my power is made perfect in weakness." ...
2 Corinthians 12:7-9 (NIV2011)

Then Jesus said to his disciples,
"Whoever wants to be my disciple
must deny themselves and take up their cross and follow me.
For whoever wants to save their life will lose it,
but whoever loses their life for me will find it."
Matthew 16:24-25 (NIV2011)

Commit and Do Not Turn Back.
Jesus replied,
"No one who puts a hand to the plow and looks back
is fit for service in the kingdom of God."
Luke 9:62 (NIV2011)

Follow Jesus Wherever He Goes.
"Whoever serves me must follow me;
and where I am, my servant also will be.
My Father will honor the one who serves me."
John 12:26 (NIV2011)

"I can guarantee this truth:
When you were young,
you would get ready to go where you wanted.
But when you're old, you will stretch out your hands,
and someone else will get you ready
to take you where you don't want to go."
Jesus said this to show by what kind of death
Peter would bring glory to God.
After saying this, Jesus told Peter, "Follow me!"
John 21:18-19 (GW)

Do What Jesus Does.

"I can guarantee this truth:
Those who believe in me will do the things that I am doing.
They will do even greater things because I am going to the Father.
I will do anything you ask {the Father} in my name
so that the Father will be given glory because of the Son."
John 14:12-13 (GW)

"As you go, proclaim this message:
'The kingdom of heaven has come near.'
Heal the sick, raise the dead, cleanse those who have leprosy,
drive out demons.
Freely you have received; freely give."
Matthew 10:7-8 (NIV2011)

"I am sending you out like sheep among wolves.
Therefore be as shrewd as snakes and as innocent as doves.
Be on your guard;
you will be handed over to the local councils
and be flogged in the synagogues.
On my account you will be brought before governors and kings
as witnesses to them …"
Matthew 10:16-18 (NIV2011)

"What I tell you in the dark, speak in the daylight;
what is whispered in your ear, proclaim from the rooftops."
Matthew 10:27 (NIV2011)

Be Loyal.
"So I will acknowledge in front of my Father in heaven
that person who acknowledges me in front of others.
But I will tell my Father in heaven
that I don't know
the person who tells others that he doesn't know me."
Matthew 10:32-33 (GW)

Remain In Jesus as He Remains in You.
"...Those who live in me while I live in them
will produce a lot of fruit.
But you can't produce anything without me."
John 15:5 (GW)

Care For God's Creations.
..."You give them something to eat." ...
Mark 6:37 (GW)

...Jesus said, "Feed my sheep."
John 21:17 (NIV2011)

"'I was hungry, and you gave me something to eat.
I was thirsty, and you gave me something to drink.
I was a stranger, and you took me into your home.
I needed clothes, and you gave me something to wear.
I was sick, and you took care of me.
I was in prison, and you visited me.'

"Then the people who have God's approval will reply to him,
'Lord, when did we see you hungry and feed you
or see you thirsty and give you something to drink?
When did we see you as a stranger and take you into our homes
or see you in need of clothes and give you something to wear?
When did we see you sick or in prison and visit you?'

"The king will answer them, 'I can guarantee this truth:
Whatever you did for one of my brothers or sisters,
no matter how unimportant {they seemed},
you did for me.'"
Matthew 25:35-40 (GW)

<u>Give Up Everything, So You Can Receive Everything.</u>
"He must become greater; I must become less."
John 3:30 (NIV2011)

" ...those of you who do not give up everything you have
cannot be my disciples."
Luke 14:33 (NIV2011)

Chapter 3

Satan's Secret Weapon

*S*atan has a variety of techniques to use on humans. However, they all lead to one mission and one strategy. Satan's mission is "Division." Satan's strategy is "divide and conquer!"

Satan would like us to believe that God, Jesus and The Holy Spirit are all separate. He would like us to believe they disagree among themselves. He wants us to believe that under the right circumstances, they will turn on each other. (Like God forsaking Jesus on the cross).

Satan would like us to believe that God, Jesus or The Holy Spirit (or all three of them together) are separate from us.

Satan would like us to believe that *if* we were ever together with The One, we are not now. Satan will pile on as much guilt and shame as he can, in an effort to entice us to believe The One would never have anything to do with us now.

Satan would like us to believe we are so far from the Kingdom of Heaven, we will never get there. He does not want us to look up and see the heavens declaring The Glory of God right above our heads. He does not want us to see or think about that great cloud of witnesses, who are cheering us on from Heaven.

Satan is especially interested in keeping humans isolated from each other. He sows seeds of disharmony from one end of the earth to the other. He tries to capitalize on any differences between humans. Satan lures us into wanting a "cookie cutter" society, where all are alike and any difference is branded as evil.

Satan understands that any parts of the Body of Christ that are functioning well together are a threat to him. He strives for division within families, neighborhoods, cities, states, countries and the world.

Children learn from an early age that winning is everything. They are rewarded for winning. They also learn from an early age that in order to win, someone else must lose. The goal is not just about winning; it is also about assuring that someone else loses. Satan loves this mentality.

Satan never wants us to consider a world in which everyone wins. He especially never wants us to go into Jesus' world, where everything seems completely backwards.

Satan has studied Jesus' Words extensively. No matter how satan looks at it, he always comes up with the same question—who wins in a system like Jesus wants??

He sat down and called the twelve apostles. He told them,
"Whoever wants to be the most important person
must take the last place
and be a servant to everyone else."
Mark 9:35 (GW)

But I tell you not to oppose an evil person.
If someone slaps you on your right cheek,
turn your other cheek to him as well.
If someone wants to sue you in order to take your shirt,
let him have your coat too.
If someone forces you to go one mile, go two miles with him.

Give to everyone who asks you for something.
Don't turn anyone away who wants to borrow something from you.
Matthew 5:39-42 (GW)

"Now that I, your Lord and Teacher, have washed your feet,
you also should wash one another's feet."
John 13:14 (NIV2011)

Jesus looked at him and loved him.
"One thing you lack," he said.
"Go, sell everything you have and give to the poor,
and you will have treasure in heaven.
Then come, follow me."
Mark 10:21 (NIV2011)

"For whoever wants to save their life will lose it,
but whoever loses their life for me will find it."
Matthew 16:25 (NIV2011)

Satan could not imagine anyone signing on for such a ridiculous way of living. If anyone did life as Jesus commanded, satan reckoned they would all be a bunch of losers.

Just one thing bothered him. Could losers together in unity still defeat his plan for division? He needed a few winners to generate envy and start the ball rolling his way again.

Chapter 4

God's Plan for Unity

*G*od, Jesus and The Holy Spirit are One.

(Jesus speaking)
"The Father and I are one."
John 10:30 (GW)

For there are three that bear witness in heaven:
the Father, the Word, and the Holy Spirit;
and these three are one.
And there are three that bear witness on earth:
the Spirit, the water, and the blood;
and these three agree as one.
1 John 5:7-8 (NKJV)

Every one of God's Creations is a part of The One. He has created us to be one.

"On that day you will know that I am in my Father
and that you are in me
and that I am in you."
John 14:20 (GW)

We cannot decide that anyone is outside The Body of The One. We are all in. God breathed Himself into every one He created. Some have not discovered Him yet. But He wants everyone to discover Him and know Him eternally.

It is not His Will that anyone perish. If we choose to exclude anyone before they have had a chance to discover God's Love, repent and become a functioning part of The One Body, we have worked against God's Plan. We should be diligently praying and doing all we can to bring light to the darkness.

The Lord isn't slow to do what he promised,
as some people think.
Rather, he is patient for your sake.
He doesn't want to destroy anyone but wants all people
to have an opportunity to turn to him and
change the way they think and act.
2 Peter 3:9 (GW)

Jesus prayed not only for His Followers, but also for those who would believe in Him through their Message about Him. The Words of their testimonies have been passed on to us. It is now our turn to pass it on to others. When Jesus speaks of those who will believe, He is counting on those in every generation to keep spreading The Word.

Amazing things happened when a terrorist named Saul encountered the Living Jesus and became Paul the missionary, who gave us multiple books of the Bible. Don't exclude anyone from the Body of Christ!

(Jesus Speaking)
"I'm not praying only for them.
I'm also praying for those who will believe in me through their message.
I pray that all of these people continue to have unity
in the way that you, Father, are in me and I am in you.
I pray that they may be united with us so that
the world will believe that you have sent me.

I have given them the glory that you gave me.
I did this so that they are united in the same way we are.
I am in them, and you are in me. So they are completely united.
In this way the world knows that you have sent me and that
you have loved them in the same way you have loved me."
John 17:20-23 (GW)

Even the person, who appears to be the most wicked, was created by God and has Gifts of God within them. Those Gifts may have remained unopened. If they were opened, they may have been used in the wrong way.

Saul had the gifts of passion, boldness, devotion to the cause, the ability to get others to listen to him and do what he asked. Those were the very traits he used to persecute Christians. However, when he was ready for God to show him how to use those gifts, all of them were turned into wonderful Gifts to the Body of Christ.

There are different spiritual gifts, but the same Spirit gives them.
There are different ways of serving, and yet the same Lord is served.
There are different types of work to do,
but the same God produces every gift in every person.
The evidence of the Spirit's presence is given
to each person for the common good of everyone.
1 Corinthians 12:4-7 (GW)

Just as a body, though one, has many parts,
but all its many parts form one body, so it is with Christ.
For we were all baptized by one Spirit so as to form one body—
whether Jews or Gentiles, slave or free—
and we were all given the one Spirit to drink.
Even so the body is not made up of one part but of many.
1 Corinthians 12:12-14 (NIV2011)

Paul continues to speak of the functioning of The Body throughout the rest of Chapter 12 of First Corinthians. Repeatedly he states that one part of the body cannot say to another, "I don't need you."

> *Now you are the body of Christ, and each one of you is a part of it.*
> *1 Corinthians 12:27 (NIV2011)*

Envision a world ruled by The One, Who always speaks in perfect unity. Envision a world where all the members of His Kingdom contribute their special Gifts, and work together in perfect harmony!

> " *...your will be done on earth as it is in heaven.*"
> *Matthew 6:10 (NIV2011)*

Chapter 5

Remember Me!

*J*esus gave His Disciples bread at their last supper together. He told them the bread symbolized His Body. He broke the bread into pieces and gave each of them a part from the whole loaf.

They each had a part in His Life and in The Mission to which they were committing themselves. But it would be necessary for them to "GO" and "DO" all He had taught them. They would need to remember that while they each had unique Gifts He had given them, they needed to stay unified in Him for all to experience All of Him.

Jesus would be assigning them to a time of learning how to live with Him inside of them. They would need to learn how to live together and feed and care for each other. Out of their unity would come the Powerful Baptizing by The Holy Spirit that would confirm their Unity and Commitment to The Mission.

Everything that was true for the disciples is true for us today. We are all a part of the Body of Christ. We each have the unique Gifts He has given to each of us. But for all of us to experience the Full Joy God intended, we must be willing to give our Gifts as He directs. And we must be willing to receive His Gifts from those we may consider unlikely sources.

When Jesus tells us to remember Him, He is asking us to do more than just simply bring Him to our mind. Through the Words of Jesus, God has given us another important Message.

RE - MEMBER!
Jesus was saying, "Let US put the members of My Body together."

Then Jesus took bread and spoke a prayer of thanksgiving.
He broke the bread, gave it to them, and said,
"This is my body, which is given up for you.
Do this to remember me."
Luke 22:19 (GW)

Chapter 6

The New Covenant

When supper was over, he did the same with the cup. He said,
"This cup that is poured out for you is the new promise
made with my blood."
Luke 22:20 (GW)

$\mathcal{W}$hat was this new covenant? From the time of Moses, people had depended upon written laws to guide them. In the time of Jesus, people looked to Him for guidance. They saw Him with their physical eyes.

The new covenant would be experienced at another level, deeper than any physical sense. The New Covenant was about Life Together, constantly with The One. It offered Abundant Life and an Eternal Life. That Life centered on knowing The One at the most intimate level, desiring to know Him as He knows us.

... "I will put my law in their minds
and write it on their hearts.
I will be their God, and they will be my people.
No longer will they teach their neighbor,
or say to one another, 'Know the LORD,'

because they will all know me,
from the least of them to the greatest,"
declares the LORD.
"For I will forgive their wickedness
and will remember their sins no more."
Jeremiah 31:33-34 (NIV2011)

"This is eternal life:
to know you, the only true God,
and Jesus Christ, whom you sent."
John 17:3 (GW)

"I will ask the Father,
and he will give you another helper
who will be with you forever.
That helper is the Spirit of Truth. ...
You know him, because he lives with you and will be in you."
John 14:16-17 (GW)

God has chosen this time to come to you. He knows you and loves you. He wants you to know Him and experience The Joy of Life to the full, now and forever! His Word is True and can be trusted.

"I have told you this so that my joy may be in you
and that your joy may be complete."
John 15:11 (NIV2011)

... "I, the One speaking to you—
I AM he!"
John 4:26 (NIV2011)

Coming Home!

"His master replied,
'Well done, good and faithful servant!
You have been faithful with a few things;
I will put you in charge of many things.
Come and share your master's happiness!'"
Matthew 25:23 (NIV2011)

And I heard a loud voice from the throne saying,
"Look! God's dwelling place is now among the people,
and he will dwell with them.
They will be his people,
and God Himself will be their God."
Revelation 21:3 (NIV2011)

He who was seated on the throne said,
"I am making everything new!"
Then he said,
"Write this down,
for these words are trustworthy and true."
Revelation 21:5 (NIV2011)

Chapter 1

The Time of God's Coming!

*G*od, Jesus and The Holy Spirit were One from the beginning, are, and ever shall be. All of God's Creations were one with Him from their beginning, are and ever shall be.

It is God's Desire that every one of His Creations know Him in the most intimate way and allow Him to live and work through them. He has given each talents, which were specifically designed to be important parts of the whole Body of Christ.

It is God's Desire that every one of His Creations live in unity with The One and in harmony with every other of His Creations.

God will continue to call out to those living in darkness, imploring them to allow Him to turn on His Light within them. He will give them time to respond. He will continue to give them Gifts of Love and Mercy, even if they do not acknowledge His Gifts.

However, there will come a day when evil will be separated out from Good, not by human choice, but at the Direction of The Lord Himself. Eternal Life will be granted to all, but where that Life is spent will depend upon whether we have chosen to truly know The One.

(Jesus speaking to His Father)
"This is eternal life: to know you,
the only true God, and Jesus Christ, whom you sent."
John 17:3 (GW)

When the Pharisees confronted Jesus, He made His Unity with His Father clear.

" ...my decisions are true, because I am not alone.
I stand with the Father, who sent me."
John 8:16 (NIV2011)

"For this reason I told you that you'll die because of your sins.
If you don't believe that I am the one,
you'll die because of your sins."
John 8:24 (GW)

The Pharisees pressed Jesus to reveal Who He was. He constantly referred back to His Father. But they did not understand He was telling them that He and His Father were One.

(The Jews didn't know that he was talking to them about the Father.)
So Jesus told them, "When you have lifted up the Son of Man,
then you'll know that I am the one
and that I can't do anything on my own.
Instead, I speak as the Father taught me.
Besides, the one who sent me is with me.
He hasn't left me by myself. I always do what pleases him."
John 8:27-29 (GW)

When Jesus was talking to His Disciples, He revealed His Unity with the Father, telling them if they had seen Him, they had indeed seen the Father.

314

Jesus answered,
"I am the way and the truth and the life.
No one comes to the Father except through me.
If you really know me, you will know my Father as well.
From now on, you do know him and have seen him."
John 14:6-7 (NIV2011)

Some have interpreted Jesus' Answer to mean that in order to get to God, they must go through Jesus. In Truth, God and Jesus are One!

In order to truly know The One, we must know ALL of Him. The woman at the well knew about The Messiah, but she did not recognize she was speaking to Him.

Many in Jesus' time recognized Jesus, but not Jesus as One with God.

Jesus grieved over those who had seen Him and yet did not grasp The Truth that they had been in the Presence of God. He said of them,

"The days will come upon you
when your enemies will build an embankment against you
and encircle you and hem you in on every side.
They will dash you to the ground,
you and the children within your walls.
They will not leave one stone on another,
because you did not recognize the time of God's coming to you."
Luke 19:43-44 (NIV2011)

Satan knew The Truth of Who The One was. But living in his world of egotism, satan once again wrongly concluded that God's Day of Judgment would be a Victory Day for him (satan). Satan believed God would separate Himself from those He judged evil and send them to satan's kingdom—a place called Hell. Satan anticipated that day with glee. He need not have. It was not going to be a "happily ever after" ending for satan.

Chapter 2

River of Life OR Lake of Fire?

*A*lthough the words "river" and "lake" both refer to resources of the environment, there is a difference between these two words. According to the Oxford English Dictionary, "a river is a large natural flow of water." "A lake is a large area of water surrounded by land."

A river flows into the vastness of the sea. All its smallness is swallowed up into the greatness of the ocean. The ocean, as we now know it, is vast, wide and deep beyond our comprehension. Micah, the Prophet, gave us a beautiful picture of how far God takes our sins away from us.

> *You will again have compassion on us.*
> *You will overcome our wrongdoing.*
> *You will throw all our sins into the deep sea.*
> *Micah 7:19 (GW)*

But, on that great day, when God separates Good from Evil, there will be no more sin … and the oceans into which our sins were hurled will disappear completely.

However, there will still be One River, and its flow will be directly from God to us.

Then the angel showed me the river of the water of life,
as clear as crystal,
flowing from the throne of God and of the Lamb
down the middle of the great street of the city. ...
Revelation 22:1-2 (NIV2011)

Jesus spoke of the Great River.

"Whoever believes in me,
as Scripture has said,
rivers of living water will flow from within them."
John 7:38 (NIV2011)

When the soldiers pierced Jesus' side on the cross, they saw the evidence of The River of Living Water that flowed from Him.

Instead, one of the soldiers pierced Jesus' side with a spear,
bringing a sudden flow of blood and water.
John 19:34 (NIV2011)

The Great River will not be for our washing. It will be Living Water to drink. Jesus told the woman at the well,

... "If you only knew what God's gift is
and who is asking you for a drink,
you would have asked him for a drink.
He would have given you living water."
John 4:10 (GW)

In contrast to a river, a lake is contained. It is surrounded on every side by land or a manmade barrier. Review what Jesus said of the fate of those who did not believe in Him.

"The days will come upon you
when your enemies will build an embankment against you
and encircle you and hem you in on every side."
Luke 19:43 (NIV2011)

Satan and his followers are going to the lake, but it won't be a fun outing. A Fire that never goes out will hem them in on all sides. They are bound for the Lake of Fire.

There will be many more battles satan will attempt to win. Some people may even conclude he is winning many of them now. But at a time known only to God, God will bring an end to all battles. The war will be over!

Then he will judge disputes between nations
and settle arguments between many people.
They will hammer their swords into plowblades
and their spears into pruning shears.
Nations will never fight against each other,
and they will never train for war again.
Isaiah 2:4 (GW)

God will weed His Garden. Those who have continued to grow as weeds of satan will be pulled out of God's Garden. Those who have refused to acknowledge The One will be separated from those who know and Love The One.

Just as weeds are gathered and burned,
so it will be at the end of time.
The Son of Man will send his angels.
They will gather everything in his kingdom
that causes people to sin and everyone who does evil.
The angels will throw them into a blazing furnace.
People will cry and be in extreme pain there.
Then the people who have God's approval will shine like the sun
in their Father's kingdom. ...
Matthew 13:40-43 (GW)

Who are considered the weeds?

> *Those whose names were not found in the Book of Life*
> *were thrown into the fiery lake.*
> *Revelation 20:15 (GW)*

> *"But the cowardly, the unbelieving, the vile,*
> *the murderers, the sexually immoral,*
> *those who practice magic arts, the idolaters*
> *and all liars—*
> *they will be consigned to the fiery lake of burning sulfur.*
> *This is the second death."*
> *Revelation 21:8 (NIV2011)*

And what about satan, who Jesus called "the father of lies?"

> *And the devil, who deceived them,*
> *was thrown into the lake of burning sulfur,*
> *where the beast and the false prophet had been thrown.*
> *They will be tormented day and night for ever and ever.*
> *Revelation 20:10 (NIV2011)*

They will be put in a place hemmed in on every side by Fire. That Consuming Fire is God Himself!

Chapter 3

Fire of Light and Warmth ... And ... Refining

*G*od has appeared as Fire many different times. Fire gets our attention. It lights the darkness. It warms the cold. But it can also consume and destroy.

When God led His People through the desert, He led them by a cloud by day and a fire by night.

> *By day the LORD went ahead of them in a pillar of cloud*
> *to guide them on their way*
> *and by night in a pillar of fire to give them light,*
> *so that they could travel by day or night.*
> *Neither the pillar of cloud by day nor the pillar of fire by night*
> *left its place in front of the people.*
> *Exodus 13:21-22 (NIV2011)*

When the people in Elijah's day were being tempted to turn from God to Baal, Elijah proposed an interesting test. He laid out the proposition and then said,

> *"Then you call on the name of your god,*
> *and I will call on the name of the LORD.*
> *The god who answers by fire—he is God." ...*
> *1 Kings 18:24 (NIV2011)*

At the end of the test, this is what happened.

> *Then the fire of the LORD fell and burned up the sacrifice,*
> *the wood, the stones and the soil,*
> *and also licked up the water in the trench.*
> *When all the people saw this, they fell prostrate and cried,*
> *"The LORD—he is God! The LORD - he is God!"*
> *1 Kings 18:38-39 (NIV2011)*

We love God's Fire as our Source of Light and Heat. However, we tend to avoid one of the other purposes of His Fire—Refining. The end result may be wonderful, but the process sounds painful.

> *"I will bring this third {of the people} through the fire.*
> *I will refine them as silver is refined.*
> *I will test them as gold is tested.*
> *They will call on me,*
> *and I will answer them.*
> *I will say, 'They are my people.'*
> *They will reply, 'The LORD is our God.'"*
> *Zechariah 13:9 (GW)*

Both God and Jesus spoke plainly of the challenges of living in this present world. They did not use words, like "you might have a little trouble now and then" or "you might go through floods and fire." No, they used words that indicated it was a sure thing we would have opportunities for God to refine us. However, They also assured us of Their Presence and Delivery from harm.

> *(Jesus speaking)*
> *"I have told you these things, so that in me you may have peace.*
> *In this world you will have trouble.*
> *But take heart! I have overcome the world."*
> *John 16:33 (NIV2011)*

(God speaking)
"When you pass through the waters,
I will be with you;
and when you pass through the rivers,
they will not sweep over you.
When you walk through the fire,
you will not be burned;
the flames will not set you ablaze."
Isaiah 43:2 (NIV2011)

Those who call upon The Name of The Lord will be refined and held up as precious in The Sight of The Lord. Those who refuse to call upon His Name will be consumed in God's Fire.

For the LORD your God is a consuming fire, ...
Deuteronomy 4:24 (NIV2011)

Chapter 4

Hell

*H*ell is often pictured as a place of fire and torment. It is pictured as a place where God shoves the unrepentant into the furnace, closes the door and leaves. That is not true!

We were created by God, Who was within us from the beginning, is now and ever shall be. This cannot be changed. We either choose Life or Death with Him.

As we have noted earlier in this book, both David the Psalmist and Paul the Missionary discovered the miracle of God's Continuing Presence.

David said,

> *Where can I go from your Spirit?*
> *Where can I flee from your presence?*
> *If I go up to the heavens, you are there;*
> *if I make my bed in the depths, you are there.*
> *Psalm 139:7-8 (NIV2011)*

Paul said,

> *For I am convinced that*
> *neither death nor life, neither angels nor demons,*
> *neither the present nor the future, nor any powers,*
> *neither height nor depth, nor anything else in all creation,*
> *will be able to separate us from the love of God*
> *that is in Christ Jesus our Lord.*
> *Romans 8:38-39 (NIV2011)*

Will God be in Hell? Yes. <u>God is the Consuming Fire</u> that can never be extinguished! He will be in plain view of satan and every other inhabitant of hell. They will see Him up close and personal. His Light will penetrate every part of their being, illuminating clearly the wages of sin satan wants to pay them. They will hear The Voice of God repeatedly and eternally.

Because they died in their sins, their sins will be with them, including every feeling that went with those sins. I believe inhabitants of Hell will experience intense regret. They will see what it is like for those who are fellowshipping with God in Joy. They will long for the same.

They will thirst for the Living Water they chose to reject. They will long to be at the banquet table with God. The 23rd Psalm speaks of those in fellowship with God, eating in the presence of their enemies.

> *You prepare a banquet for me*
> *while my enemies watch. ...*
> *Psalm 23:5 (GW)*

They will see the table, but they will not be permitted to eat there.

The story of the rich man and Lazarus was recorded in the Gospel of Luke, Chapter 16. Jesus told the story of a man named Lazarus who begged outside the door of a rich man. Both died. Lazarus went to heaven. The rich man went to hell.

"He went to hell, where he was constantly tortured.
As he looked up, in the distance he saw Abraham and Lazarus.
He yelled, 'Father Abraham! Have mercy on me!
Send Lazarus to dip the tip of his finger in water
to cool off my tongue.
I am suffering in this fire.'

"Abraham replied, 'Remember, my child,
that you had a life filled with good times,
while Lazarus' life was filled with misery.
Now he has peace here, while you suffer.
Besides, a wide area separates us.
People couldn't cross it in either direction
even if they wanted to.'"
Luke 16:23-26 (GW)

The rich man was able to see all he wanted. He still believed it was up to him to figure out a way to get it. However, as he had done throughout his life, he was not looking to God in humility and repentance. He still did not see God, The Source of all he would ever need to live.

And yet God was still with him, as He had been from the beginning. God was The Fire that continued to burn!

Chapter 5

Welcome Home!

*T*hose who truly know The One—God, Jesus and The Holy Spirit—are bound for a place much different from Hell. Those who do not know The One tremble in fear at the sound of His Voice. Those who know Him rejoice at the sound of His Voice! Paul described it this way,

> *You have not come to something that you can feel,*
> *to a blazing fire, to darkness, to gloom, to a storm,*
> *to a trumpet's blast, and to a voice.*
> *When your ancestors heard that voice,*
> *they begged not to hear it say another word.*
> *Hebrews 12:18-19 (GW)*

> *Instead, you have come to Mount Zion, to the city of the living God,*
> *to the heavenly Jerusalem.*
> *You have come to tens of thousands of angels*
> *joyfully gathered together*
> *and to the assembly of God's firstborn children*
> *(whose names are written in heaven).*
> *You have come to a judge (the God of all people)*
> *and to the spirits of people who have God's approval*

and have gained eternal life. You have come to Jesus,
who brings the new promise from God,
and to the sprinkled blood that speaks a better message than Abel's.
Hebrews 12:22-24 (GW)

Therefore, since we are receiving a kingdom that cannot be shaken,
let us be thankful,
and so worship God acceptably with reverence and awe,
for "our God is a consuming fire."
Hebrews 12:28-29 (NIV2011)

John was granted a peek into the City God plans for us. In that time, He will bring us Home to a place that is even more dazzling than Eden … a place even more amazing than the beautiful earth we now enjoy. Satan, his demons and his followers will not be permitted there.

Darkness, pain, mourning, crying, death and all effects of a previous sinful life will be gone. We will not remember the former evil things. We will no longer have the knowledge of evil. We will only know Good. We will not dread the future. We will live The Life The One created for us from the beginning of the world.

I saw a new heaven and a new earth,
because the first heaven and earth had disappeared,
and the sea was gone.
Then I saw the holy city, New Jerusalem,
coming down from God out of heaven,
dressed like a bride ready for her husband.

I heard a loud voice from the throne say,
"God lives with humans! God will make his home with them,
and they will be his people.
God himself will be with them and be their God.
He will wipe every tear from their eyes.

There won't be any more death.
There won't be any grief, crying, or pain,
because the first things have disappeared."

The one sitting on the throne said,
"I am making everything new."
He said, "Write this: 'These words are faithful and true.'"

He said to me, "It has happened!
I am the A and the Z, the beginning and the end.
I will give a drink from the fountain filled with the water of life
to anyone who is thirsty.
It won't cost anything.
Everyone who wins the victory will inherit these things.
I will be their God, and they will be my children."
Revelation 21:1-7 (GW)

A Few Imparting Words from the Author,
Carolyn Priester Jones

*T*his book has no end. It is a gateway into all the tomorrows God has waiting for you. I'd be delighted to share in your journey.

You can read more about my journey by following my blog, *Jump for Joy*, at carolynpriesterjones.org.

If you would like to contact me, you may do either by email or snail mail at the following addresses. May you be blessed abundantly as you continue to experience the Joy of being one with The One. He is with you always!

Email: knowingtheone@yahoo.com

Snail mail:
Carolyn Priester Jones
PO Box 910034
Lexington, KY 40591-0034
USA

CPSIA information can be obtained at www.ICGtesting.com
Printed in the USA
LVOW03s0546020915

452255LV00001B/1/P